SHIPS THAT CHANGED HISTORY

Books by A. A. Hoehling

The Fierce Lambs
The Last Voyage of the *Lusitania* (with Mary Hoehling)
Last Train from Atlanta
A Whisper of Eternity
Lonely Command
The Great Epidemic
Home Front USA
Who Destroyed the *Hindenburg*?
The Great War at Sea
They Sailed into Oblivion
America's Road to War, 1939–1941
Thunder at Hampton Roads
Vicksburg, 47 Days of Siege
The *Franklin* Comes Home
The *Lexington* Goes Down
The *Jeannette* Expedition
The Week before Pearl Harbor
The Day Richmond Died (with Mary Hoehling)
Epics of the Sea
Disaster: Major American Catastrophes
Women Who Spied
Great Ship Disasters
Lost at Sea
Damn the Torpedoes! Naval Incidents of the Civil War
The Fighting Liberty Ships: A Memoir
After the Guns Fell Silent

SHIPS THAT CHANGED HISTORY

A. A. Hoehling

BARNES & NOBLE
NEW YORK

This 2007 edition published by Barnes & Noble, Inc., by arrangement with Madison Books, an imprint of the Rowman & Littlefield Publishing Group, Inc.

ISBN-13: 978-0-7607-9072-4
ISBN-10: 0-7607-9072-8

Printed and bound in the United States of America

10 9 8 7 6 5 4 3 2 1

Contents

Dedicated to the everdwindling
numbers who still go down
to the sea in ships.

Foreword

Ships, not men alone, have long possessed the potential for changing history. This has been true not only of the great fleets of the Persians, Greeks, Romans, the Phoenician merchantmen, and the armadas of Spain and England, but of single vessels or small expeditions of but two, three, or four ships as well.

Thus in the fifteenth century, Christopher Columbus's *Niña, Pinta,* and the *Santa María,* his flagship, proved that there was a New World, somewhere. Those in the Old, however, were not fully certain of its closest proximity to their only firm point of reference: the European continent. In four expeditions between 1492 and 1502, the navigator from Genoa made landfalls on Cuba, Hispaniola, the Leeward Islands, St. Kitts, the Virgin Islands, Puerto Rico, Jamaica, Trinidad, and Venezuela. He also transited the Gulf of Darién.

Columbus's achievements surely are not lessened by the fact that another Italian, Amerigo Vespucci, explored the northeast coast of South America about the same time, at the turn of the sixteenth century. That the Vikings may have reached North America about A.D. 1000 remains speculation, about which written documentation is still lacking.

Early in the sixteenth century, the expedition of Ferdinand Magellan, a Portuguese, successfully circumnavigated the globe, although he himself was murdered by natives in the Philippines in April 1521. Out of a squadron of five ships, only the *Victoria* made it back to Spain, which had financed the historic undertaking.

Nearly sixty years afterwards, Sir Francis Drake, in the *Golden Hind*, duplicated Magellan's feat. He became at the same time the first Englishman to pass through the Strait of Magellan. He plundered Spanish settlements on the Pacific coast of South America, captured a Spanish treasure ship, and sailed possibly as far north as the present state of Washington, seeking a passage to the Atlantic. There he turned south for San Francisco Bay (a region he dubbed New Albion, taking possession of it in the name of Queen Elizabeth I) before crossing the Pacific. He returned home in 1580 to be knighted by a well-pleased queen.

Five years later, Drake continued his depredations against the Spanish on both sides of the Atlantic, especially the Florida coast including St. Augustine. He rescued Sir Walter Raleigh's colony on Roanoke Island before returning home. Drake served as a vice admiral in the fleet which defeated the Spanish Armada in July 1588 in the English Channel, frustrating an invasion of England.

The English navigator Henry Hudson, working for the Dutch East India Company aboard the *Half Moon* in 1609, ascended the river that would bear his name to the present site of Albany. The Dutch thereby lay claim to the region. The next year the British financed an expedition to what would be Hudson Bay and so provided England with "rights" to the whole vast area. However, in 1611 a mutinous crew cast him adrift, and he was never to be seen again.

Yet another Briton, Captain James Cook, circled the globe in the eighteenth century aboard the *Endeavour*. He returned to England in 1771, having charted Tierra del Fuego at the tip of South America and also explored the coasts of eastern Australia and New Zealand.

On later voyages, Cook penetrated both the Antarctic and the far northwest coast of America, seeking, like Drake, a waterway to the Atlantic. The inlet he probed near present-day Fairbanks, Alaska, bears the explorer's name. However, his clumsy ships, *Discovery* and *Resolution*, could not navigate far into its narrow upper arm, which he aptly named Turnagain River.

Overextending his luck, the skilled navigator was killed and mutilated by natives of the Sandwich (Hawaiian) Islands on February 14, 1779. The sailing master of the *Resolution* happened to be a young officer named William Bligh.

That same year an American would himself write history. During the Revolution, the Scotch-born John Paul Jones was a swashbuckling naval officer who bullied Great Britain's coastal ports. He made *Bon Homme Richard* a name that would excite future generations of school children. He fought a far superior man o'war, HMS (His Majesty's Ship) *Serapis*, to a stunning surrender, September 23, 1779. This feat was the first action of an emerging seapower.

"I have not yet begun to fight!" became one of the nation's early, emotional rallying cries. Jones's spectacular victory dignified the seriousness and earnestness of the American Revolution.

Many ships, merchant as well as naval, made and altered history in the nineteenth century. On October 21, 1805, Lord Horatio Nelson, displaying his flag from the *Victory*, soundly defeated a combined French and Spanish fleet off Trafalgar, Spain, signaling before the great clash, "England expects that every man will do his duty!" It was destined to thrust successive generations of Britons into battle. In losing his own life (but not warships), Nelson, forty-seven, assured Britain's supremacy of the seas into the next century. France, under Napoleon, could fight only land battles.

The USS *Constitution*, a 44-gun frigate, was the gallant carrier of the flag during both the War of 1812 and the Tripolitan War against the Barbary pirates. The 1,576-ton "Old Ironsides" furthered the demand of the infant United States for respect in many realms, including naval. While she scored other victories, the *Constitution* would be particularly remembered for her epic battle with HMS *Guerriere*, that surrendered on August 19, 1812, off the Maine coast. Lasting fame was assured for the big frigate's captain, Isaac Hull.

The renewed hostilities with England were barely over when, in 1819, a pathetically underpowered "steamer," the 320-ton *Savannah*, crossed the Atlantic. Her single-cylinder, 72-horsepower steam engine turned her paddles but three days out of the wearisome month consumed in raising the English Channel. She was compelled to unfurl her sails the remainder of the time. Her designers, it seems, had neglected to provide bunker space for more than a few days' coal supply.

While the little *Savannah* had previewed a new era in ocean transport, passengers still preferred the sturdy sailing packets, such as those of the popular Black Ball Line. They were repelled, perhaps, by the steam-driven craft appearing more and more on inland waterways. They belched smoke and sparks, often setting ablaze farmfields as they chugged and snorted down the Hudson, Thames, Seine, and elsewhere.

These vessels were easily as repugnant as railroad locomotives, which had been pioneered in 1825 with the inauguration in England of the Stockton and Darlington Line. Its fire-spewing engines and clanging drive rods scared the wits out of women and children, while causing horses to bolt with their carriages. One- and two-car trains hammered and swayed along the limited right-of-way, threatening to derail momentarily, as often they did.

Nonetheless, there were those of vision who had not lost sight of the "Atlantic steam bridge." On April 24, 1838, two true steamships arrived in New York harbor: the *Great Western* and the *Sirius*, the first to cross the Atlantic under steam alone. By far the more impressive of the two was the 1,340-ton *Great Western*. She was amply served by a 750-horsepower engine that drove her paddle wheels to make possible a 16-day crossing.

But just to make sure, as with her contemporaries, she carried auxiliary masts. With 128 staterooms, she boasted decor highlighted by a grand saloon sporting landscapes as well as panels of the arts and sciences, tenderly watched over by Cupid and Psyche.

Owned by the British Railway of the same name, the *Great Western* was the brainchild of a young civil engineer, Isambard Kingdom Brunel. He was a little man (5 feet 4 inches) in a stovepipe hat, with big ideas, and his greatest would not hatch for another score of years.

The second ship, which dropped anchor the same day, was the former British coastal steamer *Sirius,* half the displacement of the *Great Western* and 60 feet shorter. With accommodations for only forty, *Sirius* was compelled to burn furniture and other woodwork the last hours at sea, but she made the voyage in twenty days.

Sirius had been chartered by a Connecticut-born, Yale-educated London merchant, fifty-eight-year-old Junius Smith, who with a nephew, Henry Smith of New York, had already founded the American Steam Navigation Company. It was believed to be the first transatlantic steamship line.

The next year, 1839, the 70-foot *Robert F. Stockton* became the first propeller-driven steamer to cross the Atlantic, although she relied heavily on her sails. A young Swede, John Ericsson, had patented the propeller.

Across the Pacific, history was made in 1853–1854 when Commodore Matthew Galbraith Perry led his squadron of four ships, including the powerful steam frigates *Susquehanna* and *Mississippi,* into Tokyo Bay. He had been charged by President Millard Fillmore with "penetrating isolationist Japan" and freeing at least some of her ports to American ships. Shipwrecked sailors had been treated roughly, and it had been impossible to purchase coal and other needed supplies. Perry's combination of bluster and show of force resulted in a treaty with the shogunate, initially opening two ports to U.S. trade.

In the meantime, a phenomenon, the Gold Rush in California, had renewed the focus on sail, spawning a class that would influence history by their speed and dependability. The clipper ship was a creation, as one awestruck passenger penned, that "seemed to walk the water like a thing of life!"

John Masefield rhapsodized:

> Those splendid ships each with her grace, her glory . . .
> They are grander things than all the art of towns;
> Their tests are tempests, and the sea that drowns,
> They mark our passage as a race of men,
> Earth will not see such ships as those again.

Acknowledgments

The author wishes to express his gratitude to a number of persons not mentioned elsewhere in the text or bibliography who assisted in the preparation of this book. First he thanks James E. "Jed" Lyons, publisher of Madison Books, whose faith in the subject transformed an outline into a manuscript.

Risking, as always, the danger of inadvertently omitting some who proved helpful, the author thanks R.H. Brady, deputy public affairs officer, Naval Base, Pearl Harbor; Frank Braynard, curator, American Merchant Marine Museum Foundation of the United States Merchant Marine Academy, Kings Point, New York; and E. Bovarnick, reader services librarian at Kings Point, who both aided the clipper ships research. Frank Braynard has assisted the author with several books over the years.

J. D. Brown, head, Naval Historical Branch, Ministry of Defense, London; and C.J. Earl, of the British Naval Staff, British Embassy, Washington, D.C., who both assisted with the Dunkirk chapter.

Clive Cussler who, like Braynard, has been supportive of the author's books in various ways.

Charles R. Haberlein, Jr., head, Photographic Division, Naval Historical Center, also a longtime friend and researcher without equal in his chosen field.

From the University of Florida: Gene Hemp, vice provost;

Paula Hamilton, Special Collections; and Chris Hanson, chair, Humanities and Social Sciences Services.

Nancy A. Haywood and William T. La Moy of the Essex Institute library, Salem, Massachusetts.

Donald A. Howell, President, Aloha Chapter, Pearl Harbor Survivors Association.

Walter Lord, a friend dating back to the *Lusitania* days, whose research path led, along with the author's, both to Pearl Harbor and Dunkirk.

Paul J. O'Pecko, Mystic Seaport Museum Library, Mystic, Connecticut; Benjamin H. Trask, Mariners' Museum Library, Newport News, Virginia; Daniel M. Truax, U.S. Naval Academy Alumni Association, Annapolis; and Marlene P. Ware, Arizona State Historical Foundation, Hayden Library, Arizona State University.

Once again, the author finds himself expressing deep gratitude to his wife and sometimes coauthor for editorial, typographical, and especially inspirational assistance. As a New Englander and onetime sailor in her own right, Mary was particularly helpful in molding and creating order out of an inherently diffuse subject: the clipper ships.

Chapter One

The Clippers

The world indeed had never seen anything like the clipper ships, with their towering masts, dubbed "moonrakers," acres of canvas, long, lean hulls, and knifelike prows. Under full sail, they "flew" across the waves as if suspended, a glorious sight to thrill even a seasoned landlubber.

Built to withstand the most furious gales, they were often called upon to do so by competitive captains determined to establish speed records across the Seven Seas. Some would sail into hurricane force winds with all canvas aloft until the ship lay almost horizontal to the waves. Even with topsails reefed and otherwise trimmed for weather, a storm at sea aboard a clipper could be a daunting experience:

> It is impossible to describe the roaring, howling and shrieking of the wind . . . it [the sea] struck the outside of the ship and formed an arch over her so that while we could see fore and aft, we could not see above the tops, and the air was so full of salt water we could hardly breathe. The ship stood against it for about ten minutes, when she was hove down on her beam ends. I tried to gain the weather rail and I caught it with my right hand, but the rail being wet and slippery, and the ship going over so quickly, my feet slipped from under me and I fell into the sea.

So wrote Charles P. Low, sailing aboard the *Houqua* on his first voyage as master, about 1850. Though he said his "last prayer," he was to sail another day for he clutched a dangling line and was hauled back on deck.

And from the log of the *Augustus* in 1859:

> We were in the direct pathway of the gale; and also a brilliant snow white semicircle appeared, apparently one mile distant . . . with several very bright and clearly defined broad streaks of haze . . . down which the wind rushed with such tremendous fury, it was hopeless to expect a spar or even the ship itself could survive it from moment to moment . . . seas struck under lea quarter so violently as to shake out oakum. It was my most dreadful experience in 40 yrs. at sea.

The same hurricane force winds tore off all but the foremast of the mahogany-hulled *Stephen R. Mallory* (named for the man who was to become the Confederate naval secretary). Surely all passages were not so violent, but experiences like these exemplify a long-vanished breed of salts and ship handlers.

The graceful vessels, known variously as "Yankee clippers," "California clippers," "Baltimore clippers," or even "China clippers," were built to move tea and spices from the East, hides and other commodities from Australia. They were uniquely suited as well to hastening the forty-niners to California following the strike of gold at Sutter's Mill (future site of Sacramento) in January 1848.

Making their appearance in the mid-1840s and early 1850s, these revolutionary sailing craft proved faster and cheaper to build than steamships, and were endowed with capacious cargo holds. Thus a ship would frequently pay for herself in one voyage. The small clipper, *Samuel Russell,* for example, once stowed $72,000 worth of freight, about $2,000 more than her cost.

During this ephemeral period, shipyards up and down the East coast from Baltimore to Maine rang with the sound of hammer on anvil as shipwrights constructed some 500 of the wondrous vessels. In 1851 alone, thirty-one California clippers were sent down the ways. Their names bespoke the soul and energy of America: *Flying Cloud, Sea Witch, Stag Hound, Hurricane, Sovereign of the Seas, Winged Racer, Wings of the Morning, Morning Star, Contest, Intrepid.*

The bowsprits alone dazzled as works of art, a matter of keen rivalry between wood carvers. The beautiful women who were favored subjects often resembled the wife or mistress of the builder or master, while other bowsprits represented legendary figures, birds, or mermaids.

For a brief time, the *Stag Hound,* 1,535 gross tons and 215 feet in length, was among the largest in the class. Then greater clippers came along, partly in response to the discovery of gold in Australia. One in this trade, the *Red Jacket,* was launched in 1854 in Rockland, Maine. She registered 2,006 tons, was 260 feet long with a 44-foot beam, and drew 26 feet.

While introducing a majesty hitherto unknown, the clippers became the fastest products of a shipwright. Records were set, only to be broken again in a week, or even a few days. In 1849, Captain "Bully Bob" Waterman, one of the roughest of many tough captains, sailed *Sea Witch,* a prototype clipper, from Hong Kong to New York in 74 days, some three months faster than the old schooners. The *Sovereign of the Seas* once logged 465 miles in a 34-hour period, a rate no steamship then could approach. The *Lightning,* in 1854, clocked 436 nautical miles in a 24-hour period, as if in celebration of her very name.

Later in the century, in 1889, the English-built *Cutty Sark* actually outran the steamer *Britannia* off Australia. Little wonder that one grizzled captain upon putting New York Harbor astern, asserted: "This trip I intend to astonish God Almighty!" Conceivably, he and others of his kind may have come close to doing just that.

In the early 1850s, the clippers sailed so frequently from

the east coast that races, intended or not, were inevitable. Though boastful and brash, the masters were, for the most part, friendly rivals. When in New York, they usually took up residence in the Astor House. There they compared notes, drank, and made wagers on their coming voyages to San Francisco, to China, or to Australia. No doubt in the back of every captain's mind was beating the 89-day record to San Francisco set in 1851 by the *Flying Cloud.*

There were tea races from the Orient as well (especially to England), but in the 1850s the frenzy to reach the gold fields of California predominated. The clipper trade for the Horn and the west coast, 14,500 long, tedious miles, probably peaked in the latter part of 1852. An account in the *New York Herald* of October 12 somehow brings to mind today's busy airports:

> Yesterday the beautiful clipper ship *Wild Pigeon,* Captain Putnam, hauled out of her berth at the foot of Wall Street, and sailed for California. The bark *Salem,* Captain Millet, also cleared yesterday for the same destination. Both vessels have large and valuable cargoes. The agent of the first named vessel had to refuse some one thousand barrels, for want of room. The *Wild Pigeon* has only been in port twenty-nine days, and in the short space of twenty-eight working days discharged and received cargo, and is now again on her way to the Pacific.
>
> On the other side of the slip, just evacuated by the *Wild Pigeon,* lies the Boston clipper ship *Flying Fish,* Captain Nickels, also taking cargo for San Francisco. She arrived here some three weeks back, from Manila, and it is her first appearance in this port. She is of a similar model to the celebrated clipper ship *Flying Cloud,* and both constructed by the same builder (Mr. Donald McKay, of East Boston) but has sharper ends, and is stated to be the sharpest vessel he ever launched. Like all clipper ships, she is filling fast, and will leave on or about the 23rd inst.
>
> Independent of the above, there are seventeen other vessels up for the same port. Among these are the following beautiful

> new clippers yet untried: The *Flying Dutchman, Contest, John Gilpin* and *Tinqua*. The first two were built in this city—the *Flying Dutchman* by Mr. W. H. Webb, the other by Messrs. Westervelt & Sons; the *John Gilpin*, by Mr. Samuel Hall, of East Boston. The *Tinqua* was constructed by Mr. George Raynes, of Portsmouth, N.H. She has not yet arrived here, but will make her appearance shortly, to commence loading in Mr. John Ogden's line of clippers, to which the *Wild Pigeon* and *Flying Fish* also belong.
>
> The clearances at this port for San Francisco, during the month of October, give one for every alternate day; and from the first of last month up to the present date, the number amounts to twenty, including the clipper *Comet*, and other first class ships. The whole number from all our Atlantic ports during that period is thirty-six; which shows the great preponderating commercial enterprise of New York, over all the other commercial cities of the Union combined.

A grand total of ninety-five clippers and ten "clipper barques" sailed from east coast ports for San Francisco during 1852.

San Francisco, founded in 1776 when a Spanish presidio and mission were established at the location, remained a sleepy Mexican trading station called Yerba Buena until California was ceded to the United States in 1848. Although a much-visited port, it had no manufacturing capacity nor food supply of its own at the time of the gold strike. With a population of about 800, the several dozen shacks and adobe huts that made up the town were in sharp contrast to the spectacular setting on the beautiful bay ringed by rugged mountains. By 1850, the population had swollen to some 25,000.

So crowded were the sealanes that the *Flying Fish*, on a previous passage, had rounded the Horn almost side by side with another clipper, the *Sword Fish*, as though participating in a formal race. The latter made the voyage to San Francisco in ninety days, reaching the west coast port eight days ahead of the *Flying Fish*. The *Raven* and *Sea Witch* had, on another occasion, almost touched yardarms in the same desolate, storm-wracked area.

"Ho for California!" read the ads, and up the gangplanks tumbled the adventurers, a motley group laden with all sorts of baggage and eager for gold. But few passages were smooth, or without incident in the busy, brawling 1850s. Consider the maiden voyage of the 2,000-ton *Challenge*.

She sailed in July 1851 from New York for San Francisco with the brightest of prospects. Launched only that May, she was the largest clipper yet built—a three-master boasting a towering 230-foot mainmast. In command was none other than Captain Waterman who had made history in the beautiful *Sea Witch*. At forty-three, "Bully Bob" was a fine looking man with smooth, clean-shaven features. In addition to her passengers, the *Challenge* carried a crew of about fifty, preserved food, and a full cargo of manufactured products from New England's mills. This included clothing, boots, shovels and picks, wooden and tin tableware, liquor, and even playing cards. All would command fabulous prices in the west coast port—up to $40 a quart for whiskey, $4 a pound for sugar, and $5 for a pack of cards.

Challenge left port under hot, sunny skies with the customary crowds cheering at the Battery. Those sailors possessing voices replied with old chanties of the deep. Then everything went wrong. The voyage lasted 108 days, almost three weeks longer than specified by the shipping agents. But the passage was marked by events far worse than tardiness, as San Francisco's *California Courier* reported on November 1:

> The ship *Challenge* has arrived, and Capt. Waterman, her commander, has also—but where are nine of his crew? And where is he and his guilty mate? The accounts given of Captain Waterman towards his men, if true, make him one of the most inhuman monsters of this age.

> If they are true, he should be buried alive—he should never leave this city a live man. Nine of his men are missing, and the sailors who are here declare that four were shaken from the mizen-topsail yard into the sea, where they were drowned, and five of them died from the effects of wounds and ill treatment.
>
> The scene at this time on board of the ship beggars all description. Five of them are mangled and bruised in the most shocking manner. One poor fellow died today, and five others, it is expected, will soon be in the embrace of death. One of the men now lying on his deathbed has been severely injured in his genitals, by a kick from this brute in human form. Had these poor men been put in a den with bears and panthers, they could not have been much more inhumanly and shockingly maimed. They are all now lying in the forecastle of the ship. The captain, the vile monster, has made his escape, and so has his brutal mate.
>
> It is an infamous outrage to have such a bloody murderer to command a ship.

Whatever its foundation in fact, the article, fed by seamen who had fled the ship, inflamed the port. By the time the *Challenge* was off-loaded by dock workers and the captain and his mate were ready to disembark, the Pacific Street wharf was swarming with angry men. "Bully Bob" forced his way through but James "Black" Douglass, the mate whose reputation for brutality was widespread, scrambled over the offshore side to a waiting boat and escaped through the crowded harbor.

When Waterman could not be found, the mob seized the new captain, John Land, as he prepared to take command of the *Challenge* for the passage to China. The white-haired, mild-mannered old salt was rescued when someone asked the Monumental Engine Company to ring the emergency bell. This was the signal for the City-by-the-Bay's Vigilance Committee, some 600 self-appointed "law-and-order" keepers, to hasten to the protection of the ship and her complement.

At Waterman's request, a trial was held in U.S. District Court, San Francisco. "It was the worst crew I've ever seen," "Bully Bob" testified. This it might have been. If he had a half-dozen competent seamen aboard, he was lucky. Still, the court did not uphold his charges of mutiny. Waterman was reprimanded only for "cruelty" in allowing his mate full rein. A captain of sailing ships in the mid-century, Arthur H. Clark would defend Waterman as a "humane, conscientious, high-minded man, who never spared himself nor any one else when duty was to be performed. There are, and always have been, lazy, incompetent, mutinous sailors. . . ."

The mate Douglass was found responsible for the death of at least one crewman but assessed no penalty. He insisted that he had acted in self-defense, exhibited newly-healed knife wounds to prove it. That two, three, or even more had fallen to their deaths from the yardarms was not considered an unusual occurrence; to climb the rigging aloft to work the sails was hazardous at best.

The ill-fated voyage, however, altered the destinies of the clipper and her two officers. Waterman retired in California to raise prize poultry and cattle, ultimately becoming Port Warden and Inspector of Hulls for San Francisco. Douglass, the mate, so far as records are available, was never signed on another ship. Captain Land found it difficult to obtain a crew, good or bad, for the voyage to China without paying a bonus in advance. Known as a jinx ship, the *Challenge* experienced two more mutinies—if indeed Waterman's troubles had actually constituted mutiny—before she foundered off the French coast in 1876.

The U.S. Congress had passed a law in 1850 forbidding flogging on American ships. This had been inspired in part by Richard Henry Dana's *Two Years Before the Mast*, published a decade earlier, graphically depicting abuses to the crews on merchant ships. Nevertheless, clipper masters continued, as Waterman, to act as though there was no such Federal law on the books.

On the other hand, merchant and even naval crews largely represented the dregs of the waterfront. Often sick in mind and body, they went to sea because no employer on land would have them. Some were literally kidnapped from waterfront bars and brothels by "crimps" and carried aboard insensate from alcohol or worse. Many, if not most, were like wild, caged animals who contemplated mutiny as a way of life. They were not even deterred by threats of being hanged from a yardarm, as rumor had it that some actually were.

Log entries are replete with examples of punishment without which clipper masters felt they could not complete their voyages. The *Flying Cloud* quit New York a day after the *Challenge* and sailed through the Golden Gate sixteen days ahead of the latter. Among Captain Josiah Creesy's entries, exactly reproduced:

> July 11—very severe thunder and lightning, double-reefed topsails, split fore and main-topmast stay sails. At 1 P.M. discovered mainmast had sprung. Sent down the royal and topgallant yards and studding sail booms off lower and topsail yards to relieve strain.
>
> July 12 . . . heavy gales and sea . . . carpenter discovered two augur holes had been boared in the Deck close to the after sill of the fore Castle & to the side, under the after birth, which has been done by some one of the sailors, on Enquiry found the man under whose birth the hole was had been seen coming out of the fore Castle with an auger in his hand; put him in irons—Also a man who was seen to work with a marling spike which led to its discovery—them holes are about 3½ or 4 inches apart and the intervening space Dug away to all appearances with a marline spike making one Large hole.

The miscreantes were clapped in irons, but the next day Creesy wrote:

> July 13—let men out of irons in consequence of wanting their

> services with the understanding that they would be taken care of on arriving at San Francisco.

Captain Low, now of the *N. B. Palmer,* was beset with even worse troubles. He would recall that on a voyage in 1852, after leaving New York, "a man by the name of Dublin Jack" ("Dublin" being a favorite pseudonym among sailors) had knocked down the second mate with a handspike while another, who called himself "Lemons," had shot the first mate through the leg. Armed with a musket, Low had both men put in irons. By happenstance, two English surgeons were aboard and treated the injured mates. But the master made the mistake of letting Dublin Jack out of irons.

The next morning, pistol in hand, Low stretched a rope across the deck and told his crew (thirty able seamen, six ordinary, and four boys) that he'd shoot any man who stepped across the line.

When Dublin Jack put one leg over the barrier, Low would recall that he

> went for him at once, caught him by the throat, carried him nearly fifty feet and landed him on the quarter deck, put the irons on him quick as a flash and lashed him to the mizzenmast. Then I had Lemons taken out of the after hatch and triced up the mizzen-rigging, and told the second mate to give him four dozen lashes with a piece of ratline stuff. He refused, saying he had never done such a thing. Neither had I, but it was no time to falter, and I told him to give me the rope, and I thrashed Lemons well, for I was angry at him and angry at the second mate for not supporting me. He was then taken down and put in the after hatch, and then Dublin Jack had his turn. I told him for knocking the second mate down, and because I wanted to.
>
> After the thrashing was over I went forward and told the men if they were not satisfied with the morning's work, to step out one by one and I would thrash the whole of them.

> Fortunately for me, none of them wanted to try it, but there is nothing like a show of strength. I then sent them to breakfast. After they had eaten their breakfast I turned all hands to and worked them til I found there was no more mischief in them, when I let them have their watch and watch, and everything was quiet.
>
> But I had a hard time of it. Mr. Haines, the mate, was laid up for eighteen days, and the second and third mates were of little account, so that I had to keep the deck almost constantly. The weather was fearful; storm after storm with high seas and snow, rain and hail, kept me on deck and for eighteen days I did not sleep below, but tumbled down in the corner of the house on deck in my wet clothes, and got only a few hours' sleep during the 24. . . . yet my wife in all these troublous times never gave a sign of fear, but was braver than any man in the cabin.

Low had brought his nineteen-year-old bride, Sarah, with him. This was not unusual among sailing ship captains. Mrs. Josiah Creesy was often a passenger. Mary Wakeman, wife of Edgar Wakeman of the *Adelaide,* bore two children at sea, while Mrs. Brown gave birth to a son aboard the *Black Prince.* Mrs. Andrews of the *Red Gauntlet,* Mrs. Babcock of the *Young American* and Mrs. Very of the *Hurricane* were among the other seagoing clipper wives.

Yet another, twenty-one-year-old Mary Ann Patten, was faced with a most unusual challenge. In 1856, somewhere off the Chilean coast her twenty-nine-year-old husband Joshua Patten, commanding the 1,616-ton *Neptune's Car,* was stricken with a mysterious, disabling ailment which left him almost blind. To worsen matters, he had relieved the first mate of his duties, accusing him of insubordination and possibly mutinous intentions. While he promoted the second mate to the duties of first, the desperately ill master let it be understood that his wife was actually to be in command. No newcomer to the sea, she had sailed previously to China and

England. Alternately nursing her husband and checking on the progress of *Neptune's Car,* she brought the clipper through Cape Horn gales and into San Francisco ten days ahead of the *Intrepid,* which had sailed from New York with her.

There she turned *Neptune's Car* back to her owners, Foster and Nickerson's Line, and embarked with her sick husband on the steamer *George Law* for New York. A reporter for the New York *Daily Tribune* found her and recounted the eventful voyage in its edition of February 18, 1857. The writer described Mary Ann as of "medium height, with black hair, large, black, lustrous eyes, and very pleasing features."

Her ministrations were for naught. Joshua Patten died on July 29 of that year in the Lunatic Hospital, Somerville, Massachusetts. She had borne him a son only in March. But Mary Ann did not long survive her husband. She succumbed to tuberculosis four years later in Boston.

Perhaps the seeming endlessness of the journeys, even though clippers were faster than the old brigs, had something to do with shattering the equilibrium of passengers and crewmen alike—and, indeed, with the health of all on board. Three months, fleet by the measure of the old packets, still added up to a very long voyage. Monotony became the common denominator, a shared torment. Nerves were stretched to the snapping point, especially as very few clippers were designed primarily for paying passengers. In the minority were those with individual dining saloons or private cabins.

If winds were light for protracted periods, both captains and mates tended to pace the decks "like enraged lions," by the description of one traveler. Returning the simile, a captain avowed, "I'd rather ship a cargo of wild animals than you folks!" One particularly distraught passenger, wishing desperately that he had never heard of the gold rush, offered a $10 reward for an untold joke or some personal recollection not already recounted time and again. Later, this individual, almost beside himself with frustration, repeated the same bonus for anyone who consistently did not converse with him at all.

Passengers tried dances until they tired of these. The proportion of women was usually unfavorable, and those women on board generally had husbands who did not care to share them. Church services on Sunday also met with an indifferent reception. The captain or an unlikely volunteer proved a dubious substitute for a man of the cloth, although some adventurous ministers and missionaries booked passage. The argonauts read books, magazines, and old newspapers until these literally crumbled in their hands. Crudely printed weekly newspapers appeared aboard some clippers. Card playing, fishing when becalmed, and even palm readings were organized. Some took to drink, brawled with the sailors, and found themselves in irons. Passengers were also subject to punishment—including being tied to the ratlines—if they consumed more than their daily ration of one gallon of water (measured out by the ship's carpenter). Trying to climb the rigging, if not a member of the crew, was also an offense.

Food invariably ran low, even with such major ports of call as Savannah, Rio, Valparaiso, and others en route to California. The chicken coops usually were empty within two weeks of sailing. Salt pork or salt cod and "bully" (pickled) beef, while in good supply, became less and less appetizing as the days droned on. All could blister the mouth and tongue and provoke insatiable thirsts. (Hypertension from an excessive intake of salt was not diagnosed in those days.) Once in a while women were permitted to help out in the galley. This expediency more often than not improved the menus.

Most passengers packed along their own chocolate cubes, pickles, cheese, bread, sardines, and canned meat. The bread became moldy and the poorly sealed meat tins often exploded after a certain time. The masters themselves ordered "tinned meat hunts." It was a race to see if the cans would burst, like small bombs when they hit the cold waters. Sometimes sharks jumped after them—to their abiding regret.

One traveler complained of "Isthmus-made molasses with dirt, gravel and sticks in it besides some curious looking things I did not exactly understand." The first allusion was to the Isthmus of Panama where some hardy pioneers had disembarked to make the long trek across Panama in the hopes of taking new passage on the Pacific side. They were faced with heat, quicksand, snakes, insects, and diseases such as cholera, not to mention savage Indians and highwaymen in the jungles. Discarded baggage and clothing marked their trails of bone-weary exhaustion. No wonder that some likened the gold rush to wartime operation.

For that matter, any number of males set forth as though they really were going into battle. Elliott W. Cook, of Lockport, New York, listed among his personal luggage "one rifle, two holster pistols, one half-cocking same and three knives."

Loneliness was as well chronicled by Cook, who noted in his diary, "dreampt of Her last night, of my wife in her girlish days." Later, he recorded a common lament, "am getting very dirty from using salt water to wash with."

The passengers were not the only ones who rushed off to the goldfields. Once the ships reached port, they were followed by the crews, who in some cases did not wait long enough to stow the sails and be paid off. "Many of these vessels," according to Captain Clark, "never left the harbor; over one hundred were turned into store ships, while others were converted into hotels, hospitals, and prisons, or gradually perished by decay."

Those abandoned did not include the clippers because of their value and the fact that they were owned by substantial East Coast firms. However, all masters had a very difficult time filling out their complements on quitting San Francisco, resorting sometimes even to bailing prisoners out of jail. Thus, while the captains were buying "bodies," they were also assuring themselves trouble, perhaps even mutinies.

Considering the great number of passengers carried by the clippers, only a very few bothered, afterwards, to publish the diaries that numbers of them kept, if only to break the boredom. One was Mary Matthews Bray, the daughter of Captain George Bray of Boston, who enjoyed a voyage of more than a year aboard the *National Eagle* from Boston to New Orleans, to England and India, and home again. Though Mary did not state the year, it is believed the 1,095-ton clipper departed East Boston in December 1858. Much of her diary is devoted to descriptions of her ports of call and her activities there. These excerpts give a detailed picture of life aboard the clipper as her journey progressed:

> On board of her, as she glided away, in the waning light of the short winter afternoon, were the Captain; three officers or mates, designated as first, second and third; a carpenter; a steward; a cook; a crew of twenty or more men known as "sailors before the mast"; and four younger men, called boys to distinguish them from the men of the crew. There were also two passengers, my sister and myself—daughters of the Captain. . . .
>
> The Captains of these Clipper Ships—it may be said here, as it has been said many times elsewhere—were not in any way like the "Skippers" one finds in most tales of the sea. They were not bullies on the ocean, nor boors on the land. They were men of energy, of courage and decision, as must needs be, since they had to cope not only with fierce gales and storm-tossed waves, but also with the rough, and at time riotous, men of whom the crews were usually composed. They were also men of poise and polish, with a wide knowledge of the world—its many countries, its varying codes and customs.

Obviously, Mary was prejudiced. Still, stern disciplinarians though the masters needed to be, probably few were bullies. Strict protocol was certainly observed aboard the *National Eagle:*

> We went down to breakfast which was served in the forward cabin. The Captain and first mate, Mr. B—. were at the table with us. We were waited upon by the steward. A strict code of etiquette is maintained on board these ships. The second and third mates and the carpenter are served at our table after we are through. The steward eats in his pantry; the cook in his galley. The men of the crew, and the boys, have their meals, in fine weather, on the forward part of the deck. When there is a storm, they are served in their quarters. No one ever enters the after cabin, and the state rooms which open into it, except the Captain; any passengers who may be on board; the first mate; and the steward—the latter only in pursuance of his work—his sweeping, dusting and bed-making. No member of the crew is supposed to come aft of the main mast, except when on duty there.

En route to New Orleans, one of the "boy sailors" became ill. Captain Bray dutifully removed from its shelf a book supposed to be part of every vessel's library, *Medical Treatise.* After studying it, the master diagnosed the malady as smallpox and removed his patient to a more secluded area:

> January 2nd. During a sudden squall last night, the ship's foremast was found to be injured—sprung, is I think, the nautical term. When the first fury of the wind had abated, the officer, who was on deck, ordered the crew to go aloft and furl some of the sails. They refused, saying 'that it was not safe.' The officer reported to the Captain, who assured them that there was no danger. They persisted in their refusal, whereupon the Captain ordered all the ship's stores to be locked up, telling them, that—'if they would not work, they should not eat.' An hour or two later, becoming hungry, I

> suppose they decided to obey orders, going aloft, furling the sails, and returning without accident or injury to any one, thereby verifying the statement of those in authority.
>
> January 3rd. Writing is difficult today. I have to grasp my paper with one hand, my pen with the other, and brace my knees against the table, lest we all part company.
>
> January 4th. Mr. W.—, the second mate, reported to the Captain this morning that the men of the crew were aft, en masse, complaining of their bread—the hard-tack—of which large quantities are always included in a ship's stores. The Captain went forward on the upper deck, and stood facing them, some twenty or more men.
>
> "Of what do you complain?" he asked. "The bread is not fit to eat," they replied. The Captain sent for a sample, examined it, tasted it, and then told them that it was "all right." "It is much better than you will be likely to get on the next ship in which you may go," he added.
>
> But they still insisted that it was bad. "If we can't have decent food, we won't work . . . and you may get your ship to New Orleans the best way you can."

Bray's powers of persuasion apparently were great. The crew ate what was put out, and the *National Eagle* did reach New Orleans. There the ailing sailor was removed at quarantine. Since no one else became sick, the diagnosis probably was in error. Most of the crew signed off anyhow. The clipper remained in the Louisiana port the better part of January and February while cotton was presumably being loaded and repairs made to the "sprung" mast.

The Bray sisters were very disappointed that the Mardi Gras was just warming up as the clipper was "steaming down the Mississippi" for England on February 21. At sea, five days later, the *Eagle* narrowly missed colliding at night with a small schooner, from which an angry voice bawled, "Why don't you keep a better lookout?"

March 1st—Weather mild, more like April than March. M—. and I have spent hours on deck. We have been interested in the songs and Chanties of the sailors. The crew we had on the passage to New Orleans did not appear to be in a musical mood. Perhaps they were oppressed by the dread of a contagious disease. This crew sing as an accompaniment of certain kinds of work, such as pulling ropes or weighing anchor, and almost invariably when pumping. Some of the men have good voices, and all seem to enjoy it. It is not always easy to distinguish the words, and they are not specially interesting. What they sing is usually a sort of refrain, repeated over and over, but it is done with a heartiness that renders it enticing. When pulling ropes they sing this, or something similar.

"Way, haul away,
Haul away the bowline;
Way haul away; haul away Joe."

March 5th. Heavy gale last night, and the ship rolling. Couldn't sleep. Every one whom I know, or have known, seemed to pass before me during the night. Heard the tramp, tramp of the men on deck, and wondered how they could keep on their feet. . . .

March 13th. An unusually pleasant day for this trip. The waves have had a gleeful dash, as though they were at play. Mr. B—. the first mate had some trouble with the men of the crew today, during which he received a wound on his head.

Whatever might have been brewing was effectively scotched by the master and mate visibly arming themselves with pistols, "an ominous look," in Mary's estimation. Chanties one day, rumblings of mutiny the next, this seemed to be a constant on sailing ships.

The *Eagle* docked in Liverpool twenty-eight days out of New Orleans, "a short passage!" in the words of the chronicler. Until early May, Mary and her sister, sometimes accompanied by their father, were like any tourists. Once, they took the train to London, where they marveled at the venerable seat of Empire.

It so happened that in that year, 1859, work had commenced on the ambitious Suez Canal. Until it was finished ten years later, ships would continue on the long, rough passage around the tip of Africa. July 4 was celebrated en route to India near the Cape of Good Hope. Mary continued:

> The waves have run high, and the decks have been flooded. One great wave broke over the side of the ship with such force and volume, that it tore off the lower and top-gallant bulwarks, stove one of the boats, and knocked the main hatchhouse into a shapeless mass of wreckage. Several sails were split and blown away. This is perhaps to be expected since we are now in Southern latitude and it is winter here.
>
> M—. and I have amused ourselves by feeding the Cape Pigeons. Large flocks of them fly about the ship or follow in her wake, greedily eating all that is thrown to them. We feed them with hard bread, of which there seems to be an unlimited supply. The steward and cook, doubtless, throw them all the scraps from the table.
>
> July 18th. The days since I last wrote have been uncomfortable ones, made so by cold weather, the tossing of turbulent waves, and by more or less smoke from the stove in the cabin. We have managed however to do some sewing and much reading. We had another storm last night. This morning we are in the longitude of the Cape of Good Hope. The name has an auspicious sound. It should be, one would think, a name of happy omen. There is a tradition however that it was formerly called the Cape of Storms.
>
> It would seem that Lieutenant [Matthew Fontaine] Maury of the United States Navy, has done much to make this change of name an appropriate one. In his study of winds and ocean currents, he rendered an important service by his careful research in this matter of rounding the Cape of Good Hope. Instead of sailing near it, as ships had been in the habit of doing, he advised them, especially on the outward trip, to run

westward, thus falling in with the prevailing westerly winds, and then south to 48° thereby rounding the Cape, considerably below the former route. It isn't a holiday pastime even now, I judge, from the buffetings we have had, and are still having, but it is an improvement, the Captain says, on the former way.

July 29. Nothing of interest has occurred since I last wrote. One day is much like another. The weather has been cool but fairly pleasant. The Cape pigeons are gradually leaving us, or perhaps it is more accurate to say that we are taking leave of them—sailing away from their special locality. Only three came for breakfast this morning.

August 1st. An almost perfect calm has prevailed throughout yesterday and today.

The *National Eagle* moored at Calcutta in late August, where she proceeded to unload a cargo of salt presumably brought from England. The clipper spent two months at the fabled city where parks, palaces, palatial residences, and swank clubs contrasted with the filth, squalor, disease, and death in the streets. The Brays were entertained royally by both American and British "aristocracy," the merchants and government officials who lived in unashamed splendor.

Mary relied heavily on the ship's log on the homeward voyage. Their cargo was perhaps tea, but unspecified. The clipper arrived back in Boston on February 2, 1860. Outlasting many of her class, the *National Eagle* was lost in the Adriatic in 1884.

Certainly anachronisms once steam and iron ships became well established, clippers were still being built by England in the 1870s. One was the sizable 1,600-ton *Sheila*, designed for the specific purpose of carrying Indian coolie agricultural laborers to the West Indies. It was a matter of economics; there was no rush, and the human cargo commanded good money. For the officers, accommodations were luxurious.

"The whole of the cabins," wrote Captain W. H. Angel, "were

handsomely furnished and upholstered in maroon plush velvet, with damask curtains, and all the floors covered with Brussels carpet. The table appointments were very replete with a full set of the best electro-plate, cutlery, china and glass." The clipper boasted even a "complete bathroom."

For the coolies, living quarters were between decks—in the hold. On the other hand, three doctors ministered to their wants, and there was plenty of water and food. On her first voyage, in 1877, the *Sheila* transported 626 indentured laborers to Trinidad; 420 men and 206 women and children. After ten years, they could claim either free passage home, cash, or ten acres of land as their own, as totally free persons. It could have been worse; they weren't actual slaves.

Master Angel had better luck on the *Sheila* than on an earlier command, the old brig, *Maid of the Mill* which ran onto the rocks off the Old Head of Kinsale, on the Irish coast.

The beautiful clippers changed history by linking the Orient and the lands "down under" with the United States, the old world with the new. They materially augmented the colonization of California. They introduced to America exotic cargoes: satin, taffeta, cocoa, sugar, coffee, lace from Belgium, cotton from Nanking, Italian silks, rum, whiskey, and cigars. Thousands of immigrants from Germany and Ireland arrived in America on clipper ships.

They introduced, as well, far less welcome stowaways: measles, smallpox, Norway (and Asian) rats, German cockroaches, Japanese (or Siberian) beetles, sparrows and starlings, Hessian grain-devouring flies, opium, river-clogging water chestnuts, and entire epidemics of fungi including the devastating Dutch elm disease.

The high-water mark of the clipper era came in 1853 with the launching of Donald McKay's 4,555-ton *Great Republic*. Four decks high with four masts and a 53-foot beam, she was the largest sailing ship ever built, indeed greater than any steamship then in service. There were even steam winches to hoist sails.

But she would never sail on her maiden voyage. A fire on New York's waterfront the day after Christmas of that year so damaged the huge clipper that she could not be repaired to her original configuration. The fierce eagle's head that would have adorned her prow fortunately was spared.

By then, the Gold Rush fever was subsiding. Steamships were coming to rule the sealanes, and if not necessarily more comfortable or even safer, they were mostly faster. Economic depression in the mid-1850s as well as the rumblings of the Abolitionists and slave owners that would lead to secession and the Civil War had an inevitable negative effect on all commerce.

Many clippers ended their careers violently. The *Golden Light* sailed on her maiden voyage from Boston for San Francisco in February 1853 to be struck by lightning and set aflame, ten days at sea. All took to the boats, including eleven passengers, three of whom were ladies; all were saved. The *Dauntless* disappeared in the South Atlantic early the same year.

The *Trade Wind* collided in June 1854 with another ship while en route from Mobile to Liverpool and foundered. In December of that year, the *Staffordshire* struck a ledge off Cape Sable during a thick fog and sank. Captain Josiah Richardson, helpless from a spine injury suffered earlier in the voyage from Liverpool to Boston, went down with his command.

The *Sea Witch*, returning from China, was wrecked on the east coast of Cuba in March 1856. Her captain, George Fraser, had been murdered during the outbound voyage. In May, the *Golden Gate* burned off Pernambuco, Brazil. Captain Gordon B. Waterman took his *Highflyer* out of San Francisco October 24, Hong Kong-bound, never to be sighted again. Rumors would persist of the wreck of a large vessel on Formosa and the massacre of her entire crew by pirates.

The *John Gilpin*, from Honolulu, struck an iceberg off Cape Horn in January 1858 and foundered. The *Flying Fish*, with a full cargo of tea, was wrecked and abandoned while departing the port of Foochow in November, bound for New York. The following year, June 1859, the *Josephine* burned in Mauritius. In August, the *Sovereign of the Seas* was lost in the Straits of Malacca. The next month, the *Mastiff* burned five days out of San Francisco. Both the *Bald Eagle* and *Romance of the Seas* sailed from Hong Kong between 1860 and 1861 into oblivion, disappearing without a trace.

The 2,500-ton *Great Northern* ran onto a shoal off the tip of India, in June 1869 while en route to Bombay with a load of coal. At least two of the crew, the steward and the cook, fell victim to the sharks during the abandoning process, even though those who had gained the two boats beat at the voracious creatures with their oars.

The survivors made relatively good progress until about a mile from shore when young seaman Robert Ramsay's boat, carrying twenty-seven including the captain, was overturned by the heavy surf. As Ramsay clutched at the craft's keel, a terrified German sailor, yet another "Dublin", grabbed him by the shirt. When that ripped off he held on to Ramsay's leg with a vice grip. Ramsay recalled:

> I could see the next roller coming and realized that it meant quick action . . . I drove my elbow into his face repeatedly, until he finally relaxed his hold. The roller came, and swept the few men away who were hanging onto the boat.
>
> I never saw Dublin again, and swam quickly away, fearing that he might reach me again.
>
> With no land in sight and over the mountainous rollers, my only thought and my only hope was getting back on the boat's keel. So, I swam back to the boat, and tried to hold on, but was repeatedly swept off, and I felt that the end was near. . . .

The agony was terrible, but I might have passed through the ordeal more easily if I had been a stronger swimmer.

Finally I struggled back to the boat once more. She was clincher built, and one of her planks near the stern was opening up. I tried to get my fingers into the rent, and, with feet under the bow of the boat, hang on until she drifted ashore.

My chum Alex was the only one who reached the boat with me, and I was so weak, I could scarcely speak, but managed to bid him good-bye. He tried to cheer me, and encourage me to struggle on, as a roller swept us away.

When the next roller came, with a roar like thunder, I dove under its crest, and found that I was not tossed over and over, and left breathless as I had been formerly. The next time I did the same thing, and this time my toes touched bottom.

Several times I was washed up on the beach, only to be carried out again by the receding waves. I was rolling around, up to my waist in water, when two men, who proved to be the mate and the carpenter, ran in and caught me by the arm, and half carried me up to safety.

When I had struck bottom I thought that everybody except Alex and myself was drowned, and that he might not reach shore. Alex, however, came safely ashore about five minutes behind me. We mustered ten, all told.

The mate and carpenter rescued our exhausted Captain out of the heavy surf.

As my shipmates carried me up the beach I heard one of them say, "Poor Bob is gone"; and I was not able to contradict the statement, but I knew that I would recover.

Twenty of his shipmates were lost in the wreck of the *Great Northern*. Many could not swim. Those who could, if they did not make the lifeboats, fell victim to the sharks or the heavy seas.

The Civil War itself hastened the attrition of an already fabled class of ships—true legends in their own time—which, if not wholly obsolete, were barnacled and sea-weary. Many of their captains had either retired or "slipped their anchors" for unknown rewards. Fourteen were sunk by Confederate cruisers; these included the *Stag Hound*, burned by the CSS *Florida*, and the *Winged Racer* and the *Contest*, destroyed by Admiral Raphael Semmes of the famed CSS *Alabama*.

Their historical role, if likely unappreciated by the pragmatic Confederate raiders, became one of the nation's most colorful bits of nostalgia. The clippers would never be forgotten.

Chapter Two

The *Great Eastern*

"The huge ship fell helplessly into the trough of the sea. Everything moveable broke adrift, the saloon was wrecked, and all the deck fittings broke loose. Two swans and a cow were precipitated into the saloon through the broken skylight."

Surely, the *Great Eastern* was in trouble, far more so than her designers could have envisioned in their worst nightmares. This was 1861, a decade after the vessel had been conceived in 1851, the year of the "Great Exhibition" in London's Crystal Palace.

Then forty-five, Isambard Brunel had accomplished all that could reasonably be expected of an engineer, and more. He had followed up the *Great Western* with a larger vessel, the *Great Britain*, which was the first iron ship designed for trans-Atlantic travel, also the first solely propeller-driven. "No paddles!" her passengers would exclaim on first viewing.

Yet ships were but one of Brunel's many interests. He had built the Great Western Railway from London to Bristol; other railroads in Ireland, Italy, and India; a 702-foot-long suspension bridge at Bristol; any number of railway bridges; the two-mile tunnel near Bath; and dry docks. He even designed, during the Crimean War, an armored gunboat for launching amphibious tanks; it remained in blueprints.

Isambard came by his talents quite naturally: His father, Marc, was himself an engineer. Born in Normandy in 1769, he had fled the French Revolution barely in time, and finally arrived in England by way of the United States. He converted a shoe factory to a kind of assembly line production. But Marc Brunel would be best remembered for building the first Thames tunnel. Eighteen years under construction, it claimed many lives; his own son Isambard, at that time the young superintendent, was almost included among its victims.

Later, as a member of the building committee for the Great Exhibition, Isambard Brunel created the giant water towers flanking the glass-panelled Crystal Palace (which itself endured until destroyed by fire in 1936). On the same committee was John Scott Russell, another successful engineer who operated an iron foundry and engineering works on the Isle of Dogs, in the Thames. Innovative in his own right, he had designed and built several steam buses which operated without rails.

With the Palace "greenhouse" a fait accompli, the restless minds of Russell and Brunel were ripe for fresh challenges. Brunel had at the same time been touting the economic advantages of "vessels much larger than have been previously built." At the same time, Russell was looking for new business at the Millwall works. On his drawing boards were plans for steam engines larger than had been conceived for any ship. All that was needed: Capital!

By happenstance, the same year, the Eastern Steam Navigation Company was seeking outlets for its capital. It had been newly-formed in the optimism of obtaining Royal Mail subsidies for the Orient, but the politically more powerful Peninsular and Oriental Line had won out. Mustering their combined charm, Brunel and Russell persuaded the company's directors to raise funds to build a monster iron ship with the capability of a 22,000-mile round trip, via the Cape of Good Hope, on her own coal. This in itself was no minor talking point since bunkering stations were almost non-existent on the long, lonely haul to the East and Australia.

As a matter of fact, both Brunel and Russell were contemplating trade in quite the opposite direction, to America. But that would be resolved later. The capitalists of the fledgling company were bedazzled at the prospect of monopolizing the lucrative trade to these distant reaches of the globe. They set about hawking 60,000 shares for a total of 600,000 pounds, the equivalent of $3 million. This was modest, even by yardsticks of the times, for so ambitious a project.

Construction commenced three years later, in 1854, at Russell's yard at a grubby spot known as Millwall, on the Isle of Dogs. The oldest inhabitants could not remember how their parcel of muddy tidewater earth had earned so unprepossessing a name. But it seemed appropriate.

Brunel, the "Little Giant," flamboyant with his big hat, wide bow tie, and ever-present long cigars, tended to capture newsmen's attention. But various others helped fit together the many pieces of the jigsaw puzzle that was to be named the *Great Eastern*. Perhaps the best known was James Watt. His company would produce the propeller engine. Early on, Russell was quoted in *The Times*:

"I designed her lines and constructed the iron hull of the ship . . . and am responsible for the paddle wheel engine of 1,000 horsepower," while at the same time crediting Brunel with the "original conception."

Her specifications merited all hyperboles: she was almost 700 feet long, with a 120-foot beam, displacing more than 22,500 tons and rising 60 feet from her keel. 30,000 iron plates fastened by 3 millon rivets formed a double hull; 8 engines and 112 furnaces powered the 24-foot-diameter, 4-bladed propeller as well as mammoth 58-foot paddle wheels. Rising from her deck were 5 funnels (3 more than average), and 6 auxiliary masts that could carry 7,000 yards of sail. While impressive, this yardage was only half that of the larger clippers, such as the *James Baines*.

She was no freighter, hence cargo capacity was small compared with her magnitude; only 6;000 tons.

Ten watertight bulkheads divided her length into 60-foot compartments, thus rendering her "unsinkable."

At about this time, curiously enough, Charles Lungley of London had developed and launched two ships for the Cape Mail Service "which will not sink under any circumstances." Like the *Great Eastern*, they had double bottoms and a series of bulkheads.

(In September 1854, the handsome Collins Liner *Arctic*, 3,500 tons register, could have used a double bottom. She sank after colliding with another vessel in thick fog off Cape Race. Of the some 435 aboard, only 85 survived. But 24 were passengers. Among those who perished was Mrs. Edward Knight Collins, wife of the line's general manager, and their two young children. The captain, James O. Luce, did not go down with his ship.)

The *Great Eastern* would have accommodations for 4,000 passengers, or about 10 times as many as the largest steamer in service. A rocking chair and bath tub adorned first class cabins, which were twice the size of the normal cabins of her day. Her grand saloon, more than 60 feet long, flaunted, Fontainebleau-like, a decor of gold cloth and flowering glass walls, full-length mirrors, claret plush chairs, and sofas of "Utrecht velvet."

Buffet tables were fashioned out of walnut, "richly carved, the tops being of fine green marble." Cherubs hailing the arts and sciences, even as in the *Great Western*, smiled from teakwood panels, some arabesque in motif. Capping the ostentation of it all was a grand piano.

Immense chandeliers would light their way as passengers trod in presumed silence through deep red pile carpeting. Gas or candles would furnish illumination though—wonder of wonders—Brunel hoped to mount an electric arc lamp, newly-invented, atop the mainmast. It was intended to bathe the promenade deck, itself as wide and long as a parade ground, in "full moonlight."

Perched high on her blocks at Millwall, as her gargantuan carcass took shape, the *Great Eastern* dominated the countryside in an overwhelming, not especially attractive fashion. She competed in her own bulbous, nautical grandeur with St. Paul's Cathedral, relatively close by to the west, Canterbury lying well to the east.

She inspired, from the start, a range of reactions: "The wonder of the seas," "A mighty home on the deep," "The Crystal Palace of the sea," or, even "A comet with her head turned from us into space." Pamphlets, published independently, vied with the press and a hodgepodge of phrasemakers for similies and, mostly, encomiums. One titled, not surprisingly, "The *Great Eastern* Steamship," lavished: "The ancients had their seven wonders, but never such a wonder as this—an iron town destined to bridge oceans and bring the nations of earth closer together, a vast floating city." This sixpence bit of printed bouillabaisse of facts and nonsense was produced by the H. G. Clarke Co., London, in 1857 and sold tens of thousands of copies. The many ads had already paid for its printing in any case.

From his home in distant Boston, Henry W. Longfellow allowed his imagination to color in the details:

> Sublime in its enormous bulk
> Loomed aloft the shadowy hulk

If not, perhaps, his finest moment, this quotable pearl from the white-bearded bard of Maine and Massachusetts was free of slander.

But not all tossed rosebuds. A reporter from *The Times* sniffed, "an impractical, impossible dinosaur of a vessel." And Herman Melville, happening by on his way up the Thames from Holland, proved unimpressed: "A vast toy. No substance." Melville must not have been wearing his spectacles. If there was one thing on the Millwall ways it was—substance.

Some six workmen died during the ship's construction, mostly from falls. One, rumor had it, was sealed in her double bottom, having had the inopportune urge to take a nap. It was a wonder there were so few casualties. The battalions of workers toiled during 12-hour days, six days a week; they were tired. Many were young boys, barely in their teens, if indeed they were that old. The youngsters tended the forges and passed red-hot rivets, among other duties. One died after being impaled on an upright iron bar. A visitor, getting his head in the way of a pile driving hammer, added his name to the increasing death toll.

Rivets and plates, as a matter of fact, were the cause of other problems. The price of both had soared, resulting in the resignation of several of the company's directors. They said the ship could not be built economically, unwittingly emphasizing their own folly in undercapitalizing the project.

Undeterred, the "Little Giant" raised new funds on his own and continued to supervise without pay. He also found time to design a field hospital for the troops still fighting in the Crimea, though hostilities would end in February 1856. Florence Nightingale was reported to be very pleased with the structure, especially its ventilation.

By early November 1857, in spite of everything, including England's normally horrid weather, the *Great Eastern*—a name which had won out over the less euphonious *Leviathan*—was pronounced ready for launching. Curious Londoners were joined by notables from overseas including the Comte de Paris and numerous diplomatic delegations. British nobility was headed by Prince Albert, the generally unpopular consort of Queen Victoria. The colorful dress of the Siamese attracted particular attention.

Pubs along the Thames were packed with customers. Brass bands added to the excitement and confusion of the moment. Beggars, toughs, prostitutes, and pickpockets proved anew their traditional rowdy presence as camp followers.

But the huge creation refused to budge from her two massive timber cradles, no matter how much greasing of the ways or relentless pressure from giant hydraulic rams. A windlass ran wild, sending those tending it spinning and toppling in all directions. Two of them died. A sightseer's stand collapsed, and more people were hastened to the nearest hospitals. Greasing, more rams, tugs, even platoons of sturdy dockhands pushing—Brunel tried every ploy known, and some hitherto unknown, for urging a diabolically stubborn ship off the ways. The challenge was compounded since the *Great Eastern* was to be launched sideways. She had already been christened—after a fashion—by the daughter of Henry Thomas Hope, chairman of the company that owned the ship. The crowds drifted away, convinced that the *Great Eastern* would be part of the city's skyline for time immemorial, like London Bridge or the Nelson monument at Trafalgar, which had been completed only the past decade.

Three months later, at the very end of January 1858, on a high tide, the colossus relented and slipped with no audience and little urging into the dirty nighttime waters of the Thames. It was anticlimactic, like a stubborn camel finally kneeling, after countless drubbings, at its own pleasure. Her launching had added $300,000 to the cost of building, now in excess of $4 million.

The vessel continued to be a jinx. Brunel himself, afflicted with Bright's disease, was in a state of exhaustion. In August 1859, he suffered a stroke after participating in ceremonies for the fitting out of the vessel. She had been purchased in the meanwhile for a mere $800,000 by a new combine Brunel had helped establish. It was known simply as the Great Ship Company.

Before the *Great Eastern*'s fabrication was quite completed, Her Majesty arrived at Millwall aboard the royal yacht. She demonstrated stamina and savoir faire. There was the normal confusion caused by platoons of workmen stumbling about the decks, trailing ropes, tools, and assorted impedimenta. Compounding this scene was something added to the expected smells of pitch, tar, and paint: the miasma from the Thames, which was the principal sewer for London's teeming millions. Dead horses, cats, rats, and other creatures floated past like so many defunct denizens of the deep. In regal dignity, Queen Victoria covered her nose first with a kerchief, then with a bouquet of flowers as she swept through the monster liner. Her comments, if any, were not recorded for posterity.

In September, the *Great Eastern* paddled, with guests, into the Channel. She was, wrote the correspondent for the London *Daily Telegraph*, "as firm and immovable as Buckingham Palace or Windsor Castle." The ship had eloquently proven this during attempts at launching.

Then, after a lunch of beer and biscuits, "there was throughout the whole vessel a sound of most awful import quickly followed by a fiendish hissing of disported steam." Mirrors and candelabra crashed in the grand saloon. A steam explosion had blown off the forward funnel, resulting in the deaths of six of the crew and serious scalding of many others.

When the news was conveyed to the paralyzed Brunel, those present would report that he simply closed his eyes "and died."

His was the passing of a very special, as well peculiar sort of inventive genius, the likes of which the world had not previously known, and possibly would never know again. Succeeding generations would stare at a window to his memory in Westminster Abbey as they wondered who this little man was.

The *Great Eastern*'s maiden voyage, scheduled for October, was postponed pending repairs in the Welsh port of Holyhead. The dock time was not wholly lost since sightseers, at two shillings (or about sixty cents) a head, were encouraged to tour the ship.

Late in October, a raging gale tore her from the moorings.

Only the skillful navigation of her captain, William Harrison and the ability of the engineers to get up steam saved the *Great Eastern.* The saloon's skylights were stove in, however, causing extensive damage to the furnishings.

The huge disturbance would become known as "The *Royal Charter* Storm" since a steamer of that name was sunk by it off Anglesea with the loss of nearly 450 lives and almost $4 million in gold. Captain Harrison did not have much longer to accept the plaudits of friends and employers for bringing the *Great Eastern* largely unscathed back to dock. In January 1860, he was drowned returning in rough seas from a routine shore visit.

On June 17, 1860, the late Isambard Brunel's brainchild finally sailed for New York from her new home port, Southampton. At the helm was John Vine Hall, a man of many talents, including civil engineering, astronomy, and music. Orders to Manhattan had been delivered to the master rather at the last minute. Some eight ports, from Norfolk to Montreal, had actively sought her presence.

The Grand Trunk Railroad of Canada and the city of Portland, Maine, had gambled heavily on an expensive pier in the belief that the Great Ship Company's directors had assured them that the *Great Eastern* would use the down east city as her western terminus. In fact, even as the *Great Eastern* was clearing the Solent and the Isle of Wight, lawyers for the Grand Trunk were preparing suit, alleging breach of contract even though nothing had actually been signed.

The passenger list, quantitatively, was a chilling portent for the ship's future. No more than thirty-five had paid, and their number included five reporters from New York and London. Eight additional were employees of the steamship company. The little group was quite literally at sea in the stretching wilderness of the vessel, disproportionately outnumbered by the crew of at least 400.

There seemed no ready explanation for such miniscule

bookings when accommodations called for 4,000. A mere surmise might have involved more fear than awe for the great iron mass, and the tragedy of the *Royal Charter* was fresh in the public mind. Surely, the company had beat the drums in advertisements, although unnecessarily because of the continued free publicity accorded by news articles. First class fare of $125 appeared bargain enough. One might speculate that the *Great Eastern* was capable of the fastest transatlantic crossing of any of the steamers then in service.

But in any case she was off. The *Illustrated London News* sent her on her way with a sampling of its more restrained prose: "The stupendous noble vessel payed off her lead tow and took her course as if she had been the lightest cutter and threaded her way . . . into the channel."

Aside from a storm, the voyage was quite pleasant and uneventful. The newsmen's diaries read much the same day in, day out. Since the *Great Eastern* brought along live cows and chickens, fresh meat brightened the daily menus. The drinkers were served champagne, Scotch whiskey, or ale for the asking. Although a six-piece band—MacFarlane's—had been added to ship's company, Captain Hall, playing the piano or the flute, joined others similarly talented from the passenger list in impromptu musicales.

All-in-all, the voyage was a money's worth.

The *Great Eastern* raised Sandy Hook on June 28, eleven days out of Southampton. Fort Hamilton, in Brooklyn, honored the unusual visitor with a reverberating 14-gun salute as she passed, while the anchored USS *Niagara* dipped her colors. By the time the British steamer was off the Battery, she was surrounded by a ragtag assortment of small harbor craft, from garbage scows, ferryboats, tugs, and fishing smacks to sailing yachts.

Too long to warp beside a pier, as well as too fractious even as Paul Bunyan's ox Babe, the *Great Eastern* was tied up at the river edges of a lumber wharf, off West Twelfth Street.

After smashing at least 5 feet off of the wharf's planking, she was finally lassoed and roped down to many bollards, stretching approximately 3 city blocks along the river.

The press, which had accorded no bylines to their reporters other than "Our Special Correspondent," continued its Second Coming typeface and gee-whiz coverage. On June 30, the New York *Times* consumed its entire front page with the *Great Eastern* upending a cutaway diagram of the ship to bisect page one vertically. For a conservative journal, it was quite a typographical frolic. *Leslie's Illustrated Weekly*, not quite so proper, depicted much of the same, although its editors had to divide the giant over two pages.

For four weeks, the *Great Eastern* was a P. T. Barnum curiosity in this city of one million, even though the famed showman himself evinced no personal interest. If flamboyant, P. T. was also canny and mindful of his balance sheet. Sightseers came from the Midwest and the South, as far away as Savannah, Georgia, to gape and munch indigestibles purchased at inflated prices from the platoons of food carts lining the waterfront. Initial admission of one dollar was subsequently reduced to fifty cents, a lure for the ultimate total of some 145,000 men, women and children who passed through the turnstiles.

Among the most interested and perceptive of the horde of visitors was the New York lawyer and tireless diarist George Templeton Strong, who had just accepted the treasureship of the newly organized Sanitary Commission. He first saw the *Great Eastern* the evening of July 4 as he was strolling down Bank Street, where she "loomed up colossal in the twilight. It was too late to ask for admission . . . so I walked home again." Undaunted, he paid his one dollar and visited the ship the following afternoon:

> She is an enormity. But the bulk of the ship impresses me less than that of the titanic engines. I dived into their depths by the help of certain slippery cobweb or iron ladders. The huge

> cylinders and piston rods are awful to behold, even in repose. This big ship, with all her apparatus of engines, telegraphs, corrected compasses, and what not, is the incarnation (or inferration) of a good deal of thought, study, and experiment by quite a number of generations.

Visitors, including foreign consulars, stumbled over rigging and davits. A few cracked or sprained arms and legs. Two broke their necks in falls from the superstructure to the wharf. Children became lost in the labyrinth of decks, saloons, and cabins.

The crew fared no better. Most drew not one sober breath the entire time at port; one was pronounced dead of alcoholism. Another succumbed to a wrench blow to the head in a drunken engine room fracas. Others were knifed and bloodied in barroom brawls, and a few vanished in the timeless tradition of sailors and the sea, never to be seen again.

On July 30, the *Great Eastern* slipped her hawsers for a two-day cruise to Cape May, New Jersey, already a favorite summer watering spot for notables including Cabinet officers, and the lesser citizenry. About 1,200 tickets were sold at $10.00 each. To make sure that the multitude was orderly and that no pickpockets had succumbed to such a rare opportunity, Sergeant Dickson of the New York Police plus four of his finest also booked passage. He was too late; some paintings and various bric-a-brac had already been pilfered.

The experience would prove something less than a happy picnic. Food, which was advertised as available at "reasonable" prices, turned out to be meager and unappetizing as well. The chief steward explained, with few believers, that a pipe had burst in the main provisions locker, leaving only half-spoiled meat and stale bread.

With most staterooms locked, the few open ones were assigned haphazardly resulting in a mixture of husbands and wives, males and females. For the younger of both sexes it wasn't all bad. Travelers attempted to bribe stewards for air and hair mattresses. When they tried to sleep on deck, the hapless excursionists found they were showered with cinders.

The summer heat was unbearable in the saloons, especially the dining. The scorching funnels were directly behind the panels; this had not been a problem in her transatlantic voyage when the cool winds had provided adequate ventilation. "A male passenger went into the saloon to beg for a couple of glasses of cold water for two ladies who had fainted from the heat and thirst," reported the Baltimore *Sun*. "After much bargaining, he obtained half a pitcher of water as turgid as the stream of the Mississippi . . . he was told there was not other water on board." Other stewards sold water for ten and twenty cents a glass. As a further insult, the excursionists could not even go ashore at Cape May, since the *Great Eastern* had dropped anchor miles out.—"the continental shelf, you know," explained a steward.

Her second jaunt, set for Hampton Roads and up Chesapeake Bay to Annapolis, was more successful, although only a couple of hundred were aboard. On August 3, the ship anchored inside the ample mouth of Chesapeake Bay, off Fort Monroe, which saluted her with its big guns. The vessel replied with her own saluting cannon. Having navigated off course, she was several hours late. Nevertheless, almost like the welcome in New York harbor, the roads were jammed with the curious, who had come from many areas of the South. "Never in the history of civilization was such an aquatic scene witnessed," reported *Leslie's*. "Ten thousand people floated upon the blue waves of our outer harbor, and hundreds of vessels from the largest to the smallest in the world rested upon its bosom at one and the same time." The brassy sounds of "Hail Columbia!" and a song composed by its conductor, "The *Great Eastern* Polka" echoed over the waters from MacFarlane's band.

A pleasant day was passed at the celebrated Hygeia Hotel, Old Point Comfort, touted as a health spa and frequented, for other reasons, by the officers of Fort Monroe. Crewmen gaped at a sight never witnessed in Britain: visitors accompanied by their slaves.

Two days later, August 5, under a crashing thunderstorm, the ship started up the bay for Annapolis. En route, she was met by a new steamer, *George Peabody*, carrying the mayor and others of the welcoming committee from Maryland's capital. Unfortunately, the *Peabody* could not keep up with the *Great Eastern* and arrived sometime after the visitor was at anchor. The committee was not pleased. Why, the members asked, had their guest not slowed down?

There were, however, far greater concerns in a fateful election year. Not two but four candidates vied for the Presidency: Abraham Lincoln, Republican, a little-known former member of Congress and "moderate" abolitionist; Senator Stephen A. Douglas, a Northern Democrat (who would die suddenly the following year); Vice President John Cabell Breckinridge, a Southern Democrat serving in the current administration of James Buchanan and a firm states' rights advocate; and John Bell, Constitutional Unionist, a former United States Senator and leader of the conservative Southern element. John Brown, "mouldering" in his grave only since the past December, would have been most interested in the contest.

Before the *Great Eastern* departed, President Buchanan paid a brief visit. It was later reported by one of the steamship company's directors, Daniel Gooch, that the two discussed the possibilities of the liner carrying cotton to England. All too eager to placate an increasingly secession-minded South, the Chief Executive was said to have thought well of the idea.

The oversized vessel steamed for home on August 17 via Halifax, carrying 110 passengers. Her master had collapsed from the strain of the past weeks and had turned over command to First Officer Henry Machin. Arriving at Milford

Haven, she was beached for the autumn and winter. Repairs had to be made to the propeller shaft, in addition to routine maintenance—for example, painting the acreage of the ship's keel.

Nothing was small where the *Great Eastern* was concerned. How many gallons of red lead would be required to cover the approximately 84,000 square feet of surface? And what would that paint cost per gallon? What must the debit sheet have shown when her bunkers were filled to their capacity of 15,000 tons of coal? This merely dramatized the unheard of economics of keeping an ocean giant afloat. Continuing port and docking charges also nicked away at the coffers of the Great Ship Company like hordes of hungry vermin. Scott Russell, one of *Great Eastern*'s creators, successfully sued for what he claimed was owed him in building and repair costs: something well over $100,000. With such operating expenses, few passengers, and little cargo, how could a corporate entity stay in existence?

Nonetheless, the *Great Eastern* made her second voyage to New York in May 1861, with approximately 100 travelers aboard.

She arrived in a nation now preparing for war—Sumter had just been fired on and was in Confederate hands. Volunteer regiments were drilling in the city's parks. None was excursion-minded any more. Besides, Great Britain was no friend of the Union, though pragmatically she had stopped short of recognizing the Confederacy. London's primary concern was not who would win or lose, certainly not how many might be killed, but how to keep the South's cotton flowing to her many and ravenous mills.

The *Great Eastern* was confronted with an interesting competitor for her coming return trip: the 1,413-ton clipper packet (for carrying passengers and mail) *Dreadnought*. Her cocky master, Samuel Samuels, advertising superior accommodations and even a surgeon, boasted he could beat the big liner to Liverpool. Since his ship averaged twelve or thirteen days, at best, eastbound, and nineteen westbound, against the *Great Eastern*'s nine or eleven eastbound, there wasn't really much of a contest. Even so, in spite of Captain Samuels's reputation for deliberately seeking out some of the North Atlantic's worst gales, his cabins tended to be fully booked. Many still profoundly distrusted the fire-breathing steamers with their overheated boilers that seemed like fused bombs. (Reinforced steel and high pressure coils were still on the engineering horizon.) The tragedy of the *Arctic* was remembered, as was the *Austria* which burned at sea in 1858 with the loss of more than 500. There was also the steamer *Central America*, which foundered in a gale off the Carolina coast the preceding year, 1857; at least 400 had perished and a quantity of California gold had gone down in her holds.

Brunel's tour de force departed for Liverpool late in the month, bearing twice the number of passengers as on her western passage as well as 5,000 tons of wheat in barrels. She arrived to be greeted with unexpected, unfamiliar good news. The War Office had chartered the *Great Eastern* to transport 2,144 officers and men to Quebec plus 122 horses. There was fear that Irish Finians in the United States might be raiding Canada.

She sailed in late June, boasting the unexpected bonus of 437 civilian passengers—the largest complement of humans, in total, that the ship had ever listed. James Kennedy, a tough, capable thirty-three-year-old skipper, was borrowed from another company for the voyage. The crew did not reflect such a good pedigree. The second day out, a small group of them mutinied, not for the purpose of seizing control, but merely against performing any duties.

Quite up to the challenge, Kennedy enlisted the soldiers, who drove the recalcitrants up to deck at bayonet point and handed them scrub pails and brushes. Since the horses were stabled on deck (while the soldiers sweated it out in the holds), the task was less than enviable. There was resistance, but not for long. The mutineers were lashed to the aft rigging. Several hours of soot blowing back in their faces forced them to the conclusion that cleaning up the decks, no matter how dirty, was not so bad.

After dodging icebergs in thick fog and narrowly missing the Cunarder *Arabia* off Cape Race, the *Great Eastern* steamed into the St. Lawrence. It had been a record crossing of eight days, six hours. She anchored off Quebec, becoming the most imposing man-made structure ever viewed by the French-speaking inhabitants. Almost two days of shuttling by small ferries were required to haul the multitudes ashore from the vessel.

She returned to Liverpool with some 350 passengers, where the hopes of her owners were promptly dashed. The War Office charter proved a one-time affair and was cancelled.

However, the *Great Eastern* would make one more crossing to Civil War-torn America before the winter storms and bone-shaking chill set in. There was reason. Neither the passengers' area nor the crew's quarters were heated. To compensate on sailing ships over the years, voyagers had brought along their own charcoal stoves, sometimes losing the vessels and themselves in the inflammable process.

On September 10, the big ship showed her broad stern to Liverpool. Aboard were more than 400 and yet another skipper, James Walker. He had been given less than two weeks to acquaint himself with the mysteries and vagaries of his towering command.

By the second day out, *Great Eastern* was butting into a mounting gale, a "dirty westerly." From a choppy sea, with picturesque whitecaps and spindrift, the North Atlantic presented an increasingly angry mien.

Long, gray combers started the big craft pitching, but no one was too uncomfortable. By noon, however, approximately

300 miles west of Ireland, the winds were howling at near hurricane intensity. The passengers took to their beds, or their bunks, and clung to the sides with death grips.

"Ladies ensconced themselves in a protected corner where they knitted and sang hymns, and food was brought 'round in huge stew pans from which those who had appetite helped themselves as best they could with broken pieces of crockery," wrote Celia Brunel Noble, granddaughter of the ship's inventor.

The weather continued to deteriorate. Rolling heavily, the *Great Eastern* lost first one, then the other paddle wheel; next, her twenty lifeboats disappeared, one by one, like big white sea mammals splashing with sangfroid, into the boiling ocean.

William B. Forwood, twenty-one years old, accompanying his father, Thomas B. Forwood, a wealthy Liverpool merchant, would write of the ship falling "helplessly into the trough of the sea," and of the cow and swans plummeting into the saloon. The latter were part of the live cargo carried to provide fresh meat, eggs, and milk. Elsewhere, two tanks of fish oil snapped their lashings and crashed down to the engine room where they exploded like bombs. The immediate area became untenable, while the rank odor permeated the whole ship.

The *Great Eastern* settled into the trough described by Forwood as though she would lie there forever as so much jetsam. She rolled at sickening angles, which some calculated must have been as precipitous as 45 degrees. Captain Walker wondered why she would not answer the helm and head into the wind. The quartermaster, lashed to the helm, could not bring her about no matter what his physical effort. First Officer Machin was sent aft to discover the trouble. This he did in short order. The rudder post was broken, leaving the rudder to slap freely around like an immense, unruly, unlatched gate.

The ship wallowed out of control. A staysail was set. The

gale ripped it to shreds. Apparently, there were few real "canvas salts" in the *Great Eastern*'s crew, despite her six masts and forests of yardarms. The captain did not try his sails again. Forwood continued:

> The cables broke adrift, and swaying to and fro burst through the plating on one side of the ship. The captain lost all control of the crew, and the condition of things was rendered still more alarming by the men breaking into the storerooms and becoming intoxicated. Some of the passengers were enrolled as guards; we wore a white handkerchief tied 'round our arms, and patrolled the ship in watches for so many hours each day.
>
> My father was badly cut in the face and head by being thrown into a mirror in the saloon during a heavy lurch. I never knew a ship to roll so heavily, and her rolls to windward were not only remarkable but very dangerous, as the seas broke over her, shaking her from stem to stern, the noise reverberating like thunder. We remained in this alarming condition.

The anger of the storm continued into the second day. One could not easily sleep or eat. It was impossible to maintain footing for more than a minute, if that, at a time. In spite of the roar of the wind and noises within the ship of furniture and crockery breaking, a few passengers swore they heard wailings from deep down, as though in the double bottom.

"The gale is still furious. We are drifting before the wind. The pumps are going. I do not like the sound . . . the water has got in through the ports and by way of the deck." So wrote one of the passengers, an anonymous reporter for the Cork *Advertiser.* He continued:

> The captain is a brave fellow and keeps his spirits up wonderfully. He is ever keeping the men steadily at the wheel, although the rudder has been gone for many hours . . . luncheon is set in the dining saloon; some cannot eat, but still many seats are occupied. The rolling—or, now, more properly

> speaking "rocking," for the movement is violently from side to side—comes on again with renewed force. The passengers catch hold to support themselves. The tables are not fastened, for whoever supposed the big ship would become so rampant? The tables give way . . . the stewards rush into the rescue, but in two minutes every piece of crockery on the tables is smashed, knives and forks fly about, and the scene closed by a general accumulation of tables, chairs, crockery, passengers, and stewards in the middle of the saloon.
>
> I return to the deck. The spar is being thrown over, and it certainly steadies our movements. But we are still in the trough of the sea.

He alluded to an old sailor's expedient of dropping a weighted spar, attached by a strong hawser, to act as a sea anchor.

On the third day, Sunday, after a meeting of the male passengers, a thirty-eight-year-old civil engineer from Massachusetts, Hamilton Towle, volunteered to help. He thought he could effect a crude jury rig for the rudder, using block and chain tackle. Master Walker, with some misgivings, assented, ordering his own engineers to assist. Meanwhile, he kept firing distress rockets.

In response to the fiery-tailed signals, the brig *Magnet*, out of Nova Scotia, materialized from the mists. Procuring a megaphone from one of the mates, the affluent Liverpool businessman, Forwood, shouted to the little ship, "I'll pay you $500 a day to stand by!" There was no reply. Next, he offered to purchase the *Magnet* outright. And still the brig remained silent, apparently not believing so singular a proposition. She stood by a little longer, only to be able, as it turned out, to claim demurrage for delaying her cargo of salt cod. (The Great Ship Company would ultimately pay.)

That night, the storm abated. Using her propeller alone, the crippled vessel raised the Old Head of Kinsale, Ireland, pushed along by the winds and the Gulf Stream. She limped into Cork harbor. As William Forwood observed, in understatement; "It was a remarkable voyage."

The young man continued on to New York in an Inman Liner, the *City of Washington,* while his father, Thomas, swore he would never set foot again in another ship, not even a Mersey ferry.

And so the hapless owners were faced with huge new repair bills and more months of idleness. At a cost of at least one-third of a million dollars, the big liner was ready for sea in the spring of 1862. She had a new master, her sixth, Walter Paton, a man nearly as short of stature as Brunel.

She arrived in New York in mid-May to be served with a $100,000 claim by Hamilton Towle for saving the ship, as he maintained, through his jury rig. The civil engineer had just been awarded a lifesaving medal. The company's agents settled for one-tenth of the sum so that the vessel could start on her return with 700 passengers and 3,000 tons of cargo, half her capacity. Obviously, this included no Southern cotton for the starved British mills, the blockade was tight. The North would have been pleased to supply the lack could they obtain the precious bales.

She made a second voyage in July, carrying nearly 400 paying passengers. She sailed yet a third time from Liverpool with more than 800 passengers and her holds full of machinery, manufactured goods, clothing, and liquor. In fact, she was loaded in such quantity that she drew 30 feet of water, or 4 more than normal. If her owners had been willing to book immigrants from Ireland and Germany, she could have packed all the living space. But, prudishly, her owners thought of *Great Eastern* as a "first class ship."

It appeared at long last as though the big craft was going to earn money for her shareholders. Breaking with precedent, Captain Walter Paton was embarking on his third trip.

After butting into a gale for several days, without incurring damage or much discomfort, the *Great Eastern* raised Montauk Point, on the eastern extremity of Long Island, August 27. On this bright moonlit night, Paton hove to for an hour and a half, waiting for the pilot. When he climbed the rope ladder up the towering side, the ship continued on her voyage.

About 2:00 A.M. there was a crunching sound from far below, followed by a rumble. Paton dispatched an officer to check the bilges. He discovered no leaks, in fact nothing wrong, even though the *Great Eastern* had commenced a list to starboard. The master kept on to Flushing Bay where he would anchor and be served by ferries and launches, thereby saving dockage.

Since his command still heeled to starboard, Paton hired a diver to inspect the keel. When he reemerged from a lengthy plunge, he conveyed dire news: The *Great Eastern* revealed an 83-foot gash in her bottom. Any ordinary ship without a double hull would have been sunk. Since there was no drydock in New York or, in fact, anywhere in the world to handle the *Great Eastern*, how would the damage be repaired?

While Paton pondered the dilemma and awaited word from the company, the next sailing was cancelled, and the crew disappeared into the ever-handy saloons, hoping to sign on another ship before exhausting their meager but ill-spent funds. One thing the oldtimers noticed: the strange, occasional wails from deep down had ceased. Perhaps, just perhaps, they speculated, the ghost had been washed out through the hole?

Soundings made, belatedly, by the Revenue Cutter Service (predecessor of the U.S. Coast Guard) off Montauk showed an uncharted ledge, towering up to a sharp pinnacle, only 24 feet beneath the surface. Since on this voyage the *Great Eastern* drew 6 feet more than this depth, she could not have missed on her course of that night. It was scant consolation for the Great Ship Company that she had, by her rupture, named a dangerous ledge: the Great Eastern Reef, a christening that would endure.

Engineers finally fashioned an 100-foot-long cofferdam, or blister, which would be affixed to the hull where the rupture was and the water pumped out. Workmen then could descend through a tube and rivet new plates. The plan worked, but four months were consumed. At the outset, bolstering of the riveters' courage had been required, not because of the depth, but because of superstition. Unlike members of the crew, they were not convinced that the ghost had been swept into Long Island Sound. So widespread along the world's waterfronts was the tale of the entombed riveter from the Isle of Dogs that the workmen swore they heard a strange pounding from within.

The most persuasive efforts of Captain Paton himself, accompanying the men below, were marshaled to reassure them that any noises were from the engines or, perhaps, from flotsam in the dirty waters of the bay bumping along the ship's length. Eventually, they were disabused of the notion and went about their task.

Even as they riveted, sweated, and swore, bloody history was being beaten out on the fields of America. The Union rout at the Second Battle of Manassas (Bull Run) on August 9 was followed by the Battle of Antietam, September 17, when General Lee was turned back at disastrous cost after an attempt to invade the Union. In the see-saw of war's fortunes, the Federal forces were repulsed in an ill-conceived attack upon Fredericksburg, Virginia, December 13.

On New Year's Day 1863, President Lincoln issued his Emancipation Proclamation, aimed against slavery in those states "in rebellion against the United States." Lincoln had reiterated that his primary aim was to "save the Union." Richmond scoffed. Most blacks could not read anyhow, Southerners asserted. Besides, this was a struggle for states' rights, not for the social status of household servants. And who was to pick the South's lifeblood, cotton, without slaves?

That same January 1, the *Great Eastern*, heavy with 3,000

tons of wheat and almost 1,200 passengers, including any number of young males fleeing army service, sailed for home. Awaiting her was a bill for one-third million dollars in repairs. It was one on which her insurers would default. Had not the owners read the fine print as to accidents resulting from "faulty navigation"?

The ship made two more trips to the United States in the summer, including one early in July when the North was reacting with restrained exuberance to twin victories: Gettysburg and Vicksburg. After the losses at Antietam, Lee had overextended himself in attempting to swing into Pennsylvania. He had lost the war during those sweltering summer days at Gettysburg. His manpower, the finest young men of the South, was irreplacable. An entire army—Lieutenant General John B. Pemberton's—was surrendered at Vicksburg. Of Grant's triumph in taking the strategic Mississippi River port, Lincoln observed, "The Father of Waters flows unvexed to the sea."

Even as the *Great Eastern* docked, New York seethed from the draft riots, in which predominantly Irish and German immigrant laborers burned buildings, including the Colored Orphan Asylum, and lynched hundreds of Negroes. Only the arrival of units of the Army of the Potomac, fresh from Gettysburg, saved Manhattan from resembling a latter day Carthage.

After one more trip to the United States, the *Great Eastern*, bankrupt, was laid up until 1864, when she was sold at auction for $125,000 about one twenty-fourth her original cost. Daniel Gooch and two others had become the new owners, even though creditors with liens still lurked in the wings. However, there was new hope: Cyrus Field, a wealthy Massachusetts merchant, would charter the monster for a new attempt to stretch the Atlantic cable. It had been six years since Field's failure, using an American and a British naval vessel. The cable had parted after the first message.

By July 1865, some three months after Lee's surrender at Appomattox, the *Great Eastern* had been fitted with the necessary equipment for the stupendous task. On August 2, she was 606 miles from Heart's Content, Newfoundland, or 1,062 nautical miles west of Valentia, Ireland. Field was optimistic.

Submarine cables were not altogether new. Regular telegraphic service already linked Ireland and England under the Irish Sea, and England to France via the Channel. There was a cable across the North Sea to Holland, plus various hookups in the Mediterranean. Efforts were underway to connect Canada and Russia by way of the Bering Straits. Lead/sulphuric acid batteries were being manufactured that produced more and more voltage and held their charge longer. However, these existing cables transited relatively shallow waters.

Carrying 5,000 tons of gutta-percha-insulated, seven-strand cable, the *Great Eastern* had put the Irish coast astern on July 25, with Royal Navy escort. Aside from routine electrical problems, the 1⅛-inch diameter cable had been unrolling from the drums into the ocean "as easily as the thread flies from the reel in a lady's workbasket." Thus wrote William Howard Russell, former Crimean War correspondent, aboard to acquaint readers of *The Times* of London with the $3 million project. The flowery-styled reporter was also known as "Bull Run" Russell for his decidedly pro-South coverage of the ill-starred Manassas battle. He continued:

> Light gray sheets of drizzling cloud flew over the surface of the sea . . . [and] set men talking of icebergs and Arctic storms; towards evening the wind fell . . . a cold clammy vapour settled down on ship and sea, bringing . . . a leaden calm; so that the waves lost their tumbled crests, and slept at last in almost murmuring slumber . . . the big ship slept not. The clank and beat of machinery ceased never, and the dull mill-like clatter of cable apparatus seemed to become more active as the night wore on.

> The forge fires glared on her decks and there, out in the midst of the Atlantic, anvils rang and sparks flew; and the spectator thought of some village far away, where the blacksmith worked, unvexed by the cable anxieties and greed of speedy news. As the blaze shot up, ruddy, mellow and strong, and flung arms of light aloft and along the glistening decks, and then died into a red centre. Masts, spars and ropes were for the instant touched with a golden gleaming, and strange figures were called out from the darkness . . . outside us all was obscurity; but now and then vast shadows, which moved across the arc of lighted fogbank, were projected far away by the flare.

The fog thickened, "it was dead calm, and the *Great Eastern* seemed to float on a gray and polished surface of a cloud." But none was prepared for a sudden change of events. Communications that had been maintained with Ireland stopped. The galvanometer showed that the electric signals had ceased. More than 1,000 miles of cable had gone dead, mute as the dinosaurs and the fabled sea serpents. Three-quarters of the job had been completed. The end had been in sight.

Now, nothing remained but to start hauling the cable in and attempt to find the flaw. This operation proceeded for several hours until suddenly the restraining gears or "stoppers" let go. Then, the cable "with one bound leaped over intervening space and flashed into the sea."

"The shock of the instant was as sharp as the snapping of the cable itself. No words could describe the bitterness of the disappointment. The cable gone!"

For the next several days, while the crew grappled for the lost cable, "all life died out on the vessel," Russell concluded. "The time passed heavily . . . the drums beat no more, their long reveille ended in the muffled roll of death; that which had been broken could give no trouble to break . . . no noise was heard except the dull droning grating of the wire rope over the wheels at the bows."

On August 8, following a moonlit night "of great brightness," it appeared that the "picking up" line, with its grapnel hooks (mounting huge flukes, and weighing 300 pounds each), was about to reel the lost cable back on board. Slowly, it was retrieved and success appeared imminent, then "the end of the rope flourished its iron fist in the air and struck out with it right and left, as though it were animated by a desire to destroy those who might arrest its progress."

Three days later and another try. At 9:40 P.M., in deep blackness the line let go again, "whistling through the air like a round shot." From the decks, a chorus: "It's gone!" Russell postscripted, "The battle was over!"

HMS *Terrible*, putting out for St. John's for coal, hove to alongside to collect mail for North America. Wind was whipping up the sea.

> It was wild and dark . . . the flash of a gun from the *Terrible* to recall her cutter lighted up the gloom, and the glare of an answering blue light, burned by the boat, revealed for an instant the hull of the man-of-war on the horizon waters. There was a profound silence aboard the big ship.
>
> She struggled against the helm for a moment as though she still yearned to pursue her course to the west, then bowed her head to the angry sea in admission of defeat, and moved slowly . . . the signal lanterns flashed from the *Terrible*, "farewell!" The lights from our paddlebox pierced the night, "goodbye! thank you!" in sad acknowledgment.
>
> Then each sped on her way in solitude and darkness.

Again, news between the worlds on either side of the ocean would consume two weeks in transit. The fall of Richmond on April 3, for example, was not announced in London until April 17. Bearing New York newspapers, the steamer

Australasian docked in Liverpool on that date. On April 24, the SS *Asia* told a saddened Britain of General Lee's capitulation on the ninth. (The next year, 1866, on July 27, Cyrus Field telegraphed from Heart's Content, Newfoundland, to President Johnson: "Sir, the Atlantic cable was successfully completed this morning. I hope that it will prove a blessing to England and the United States." At last, the "big ship" had won out. The initial rate was $1.25 a word, with no dearth of senders.)

The momentous act of laying the transatlantic cable justified the *Great Eastern*'s troubled existence and was beyond dispute her greatest accomplishment. The feat also won her latest captain, James Anderson, a knighthood. The *Great Eastern* would not win anything. The remainder of her career was unimpressive, to say the least.

First, she was chartered by the French government and refurbished with the intent of bringing Americans to the 1867 Universal Exposition in Paris. Her temporary operators referred to the big ship as *Le Grand Oriental*—what else? Jules Verne was aboard. The presence of the famed author, however, did not prove magic enough to attract much of a crowd. Westbound or eastbound, she transported fewer than 200 passengers. Another failure was recorded. The Parisian newspapers had the good taste not to mention the fiasco; it was as though the ship had never existed.

For the next several years, the *Great Eastern* reverted to a familiar role: laying cables, first for the French to their possessions, the Islands of St. Pierre and Miquelon, off Newfoundland; next, for Field along the original Atlantic route; finally, for the British in the Indian Ocean and Red Sea. At last, she had sailed to the East, fulfilling her blueprinted destiny.

From then on, it was all downhill. The ship was used as a platform for pile drivers—degradation of degradations!—and as a floating billboard in the Mersey for the Liverpool department store, Lewis's. (Lewis's newer store would be bombed out in the 1940 blitz.) The saloons and a number of cabins had been converted to pubs and restaurants, even a shooting gallery and a freak show, by the Great Eastern Steamship Exhibition and Entertainment Co. At night she throbbed from the dancing on deck to several noisy bands.

The Mrs. Grundys of Liverpool bruited with mischievous purpose the rumors of "scandalous" goings-on in unoccupied cabins. A bloomin' nest for chippies . . .

A plan to take the *Great Eastern* to the New Orleans Exhibition of 1884, fortunately, was abandoned. Doubtlessly she could not have sailed her barnacled, rat-ridden hull across the Atlantic one more time. The vessel, in sum, defied profit, like the willful, perverse, rusting, almost satanic hulk that she was.

When sold at auction in 1887, the *Great Eastern* had bankrupted seven different owners. She brought exactly $80,000 as scrap. But at long last she put her latest owner, Bath and Sons, metal dealers, in the black. Her components, including copper, brass, iron plates, and rivets, were sold for nearly four times what Bath had bid. In effect, she was worth more as a corpse, subject to dismemberment, than she ever had been as a living, operating steamship.

The *Great Eastern* was broken up in 1889, more than thirty-one years after her launching, not a bad lifespan for a vessel. Rumor had it that a skeleton was found in her double bottom, convincing the superstitious that the reports of wailings had indeed been well founded. The world had seen many changes, sociologically and scientifically, during this time. The *Great Eastern* had made her own contributions, in spite of fumblings and general unwieldiness. She had taught marine architects, both by positive and negative example, how to build a superliner. Her double hull and watertight compartments had proved their worth. She had dramatically demonstrated, as well, the debacles resulting from being underpowered in relation to size as well as the folly of building wildly superfluous accommodations. She had never been 100 per cent booked. Her best was 65 per cent. For her maiden voyage, it was 1 per cent!

But the *Great Eastern* had pointed the way to a nautical tomorrow, the "Atlantic Bridge" of magnificent liners that would alter history as well as mores by drawing the Old and New Worlds closer together. She was the "mother of ocean liners," wrote the late James Dugan in *The Great Iron Ship*. Ungainly, awkward, cussed oaf of a vessel, the *Great Eastern* had nonetheless fulfilled her destiny.

Chapter Three

USS *Monitor*

The Civil War, War Between the States, War of the Rebellion, or whatever became known as the first "modern" conflict. Breech loading and rifled guns appeared, even the first machine gun, the Gatling. There were percussion and electrically detonated mines, known then as "torpedoes," and repeating rifles, necessitating a complete bullet and cartridge, as did the machine gun. Trench warfare proved an ominous preview of 1914–1918. Amphibious operations played a major role in river and bay engagements. Explosive shells became deadlier and more accurate. The ancestor of the submarine made its debut. There were ambulances and photographers' wagons, even military railroads such as that linking City Point with Union works outside of Petersburg. Possibly the most dramatic of all was the revolving turret mounted on an armored warship, which would change naval warfare—and history—forever.

The *Great Eastern* had completed three Atlantic crossings by September 1861 when President Lincoln was confronted by a testy, often imperious fifty-eight-year-old Swedish inventor, bearing a pasteboard model of a peculiar little vessel he referred to before a puzzled Executive as a "battery." And, as John Ericsson had bluntly told a naval board, it was their "duty to the country" that this craft be constructed.

Indeed, something had to be done. The Union was reeling from defeats on land and sea. There was the debacle of Bull

Run in July. Three months before, on April 21, the strategic Norfolk Navy Yard, with its men o' war, cannon, ammunition, and all manner of vital materiel, was abandoned to the Confederacy. As damaging as the loss of the yard itself was that of the 3,000-ton "first class" propeller-driven frigate *Merrimack*. One of only six, she mounted upwards of fifty guns and was vaunted as a match of any fighting ship afloat. Worse yet, the Confederates had salvaged her from an unsuccessful scuttling and, even now, were known to be plating her with armor to make her as formidable as any warship ever built. Thus what Ericsson was describing to Lincoln seemed little less than absurd as a challenger to the enemy colossus-to-be.

The new ship the inventor described to the Chief Executive was something no more than 172 feet long with a narrow 41½-foot beam and but one battery of guns. Her tonnage would be no less than 776 and no more than 990. The armament, her tour de force, would be particularly unique: a revolving armored turret mounting two big cannon. The hull would be composed wholly of ⅜-inch iron plates. The side armor, actually a protecting "raft" extending partly below the waterline, would consist of five layers of 1-inch plates against more than 2 feet of oak, while two layers of ½-inch plate hammered onto timber would compose the armored deck of the "raft." Since this singular warship would ride so low in the water, its inventor saw small chance of direct hits on deck. Scant wonder that Commander Charles H. Davis of the Navy's august Bureau of Yards and Docks had derided it as being "in the image of nothing in the heaven above or the earth beneath or in the waters under the earth!"

Undaunted, Ericsson assured Lincoln, "The sea shall ride over her and she shall live in it like a duck." He had come to the right man, albeit no ordnance expert. "All I have to say," quipped Lincoln, "is what the girl said when she stuck her foot into the stocking: 'It strikes me there's something in it!' "

In three days, Ericsson and his partners held a contract for

$275,000 to build what the Swede dubbed a "Monitor." Keel would be laid within six weeks.

As an armored warship, however, the inventor's brainchild was not wholly a first. In the sixteenth century, Admiral Yi of Korea fabricated his little metal-topped "turtle ships," propelled by rowers. Much more contemporaneously, as the 1850s drew to a close, both France and Great Britain could each boast an iron-armored war vessel. HMS *Warrior*, the larger, was a mammoth 9,200-ton juggernaut, 380 feet long. Similar ironclads, including HMS *Black Prince*, were on the ways and drawing boards. The French tricolor flew from a smaller, less formidable *Gloire*.

Revolving turrets had long been a gleam in other inventors' eyes. At the turn of the nineteenth century, England and France, glowering ferociously at one another across the English Channel, both possessed drawings of "castle towers" mounting clumsy cannon which were to be placed on barges. In 1841, Theodore R. Timby, an otherwise obscure inventor, offered a disinterested U.S. War Department a true moving turret with ports for guns. He did not patent it until two decades later.

But John Ericsson was the first to combine several concepts to produce a working, modern man o' war. Indeed, he had been at the drawing board in his native Sweden since the age of ten—in 1813—when he was creating excellent diagrams, including one of a complex sawmill and pump. When not quite thirteen, he had been commissioned to produce drawings for the Gota Canal Company. Barely into his twenties, Ericsson devised a means whereby the entire engine system of Sir John Ross's Arctic expedition ship *Victory* could be placed below waterline. This was an innovation, but not a happy one.

Apparently, the machinery did not work well. Searching for a Northwest Passage, Ross became so dissatisfied with Ericsson's handiwork that he ordered it torn loose and dumped overboard and returned to the use of sails. Truly a poor loser,

Ross threatened the inventor with a duel. This was prevented by cooler heads.

Undaunted, Ericsson built a locomotive, the *Novelty*, to compete with George Stephenson's already famous *Rocket*. The Swede's engine proved the fastest thing on tracks in 1829—so fast that it hit an unheard of 60 miles per hour before bursting into bits in front of horrified throngs.

Like any prudent European facing reverses in his native clime, Ericsson decided to leave for America. This he did in 1839, taking passage on Brunel's *Great Western*. He had been working on the rotary or screw propeller, a principle perceived by Archimedes two centuries before Christ. Convinced that paddle wheels were both inefficient and antediluvian, he had been unable to persuade engineers of the Royal Navy, who had laughed at him. In New York, he continued his probing.

The Americans were more receptive. He soon had five propeller-driven steamers cutting through the Great Lakes and the Chesapeake and Delaware Canal. He then installed the propeller on a 600-ton frigate of his design, the USS *Princeton*. Unfortunately, it would turn out, he allowed a British friend and sometimes partner, Robert F. Stockton, to create and place on deck a monster 12-inch gun, nicknamed the "Peacemaker."

On February 28, 1844, President John F. Tyler and a party of notables boarded the warship in the Potomac River for a firing demonstration. The big gun blew up, killing five of those witnessing the event, including two cabinet officers. Although Ericsson had not designed the improperly reinforced weapon, the Navy refused to pay him some $14,000 still owed for the *Princeton*.

Ericsson turned to other projects: inventing his "caloric" engine, a steam-type powered by hot air; perfecting propellers and defending challenges to his patents on them; drawing innumerable blueprints for ships that could not yet be found on any ocean or waterway. For the better part of two decades, Ericsson was an almost forgotten bachelor and inventor living in a large, echoing mansion on Beach Street in lower Manhattan. His wife Amelia had returned to England out of lonely, desperate boredom. What did he need of a woman, anyhow, with all his blueprints, other paraphernalia and models (some working) of this and that? The place was cluttered enough as it was.

Then, destiny caught up with this difficult, often arrogant man. All at once, he was a familiar, shambling figure in the Greenpoint section of Brooklyn, where his *Monitor* was growing in the metallic womb of Thomas Rowland's Continental Iron Works. This was the core for some ten other yards and shops where components such as machinery, piping, and the wonderful turret were being forged and hammered out.

The turret, certainly, was the whole reason for this curious little vessel. Being created by the Novelty Iron Works, it had a 20-foot inside diameter and was 9-feet high, with 8 inches of armor, for a total weight of 120 tons. Twin 11-inch Dahlgren smoothbores would protrude from oval gunports, 6 feet above the deck. Also known as "columbiads," these heavy, reinforced cannon fired 184-pound shot, propelled by 15 pounds of powder. Resting on a flat bronze ring, the turret was connected by a central vertical shaft and gears to a 25-horsepower steam engine below decks, controlled by one man. Other than the turret, only the telescoping funnel and a small boxlike pilot house were above deck.

Other innovations included an oversize 9-foot-diameter propeller, shielded well under the stern and driven by twin horizontal steam engines of Ericsson's design developing 320 horsepower; forced air ventilation (since all the crew of fifty lived below waterline); and a toilet flushed by compressed air.

Meanwhile, during the early winter of 1861–62, the *Merrimack*, to be renamed CSS (Confederate States Ship) *Virginia*, was taking shape in the Gosport, or Norfolk, Navy Yard. She bore scant resemblance to her original configuration. The frigate's superstructure had been cleaned away to make room for a 172-foot heavily armored, sloping housing with 10 gunports. The heaviest cannon would be 9-inch Dahlgrens, also captured from the U.S. Navy. Two layers of 1- and 2-inch-thick rolled railroad iron plates were laid upon the housing or casemate's 2 feet of oak-pine.

Thus, almost 1,000 tons were added to the *Merrimack*'s designed 3,000. It would create a draft of no less than 22 feet and immeasurably strain her already failing engines. She had been in the yard initially for new engines as well as a new shaft.

No wonder that one who would serve aboard her, Lieutenant John Taylor Wood of the Confederate Army, snorted that *Merrimack* "was as unwieldy as Noah's Ark!" At that, he may have denigrated the maneuverability of Father Noah's tour de force.

The little *Monitor* was launched first, on January 30, 1862, during a cold winter rain. Ericsson himself stood near the stern to demonstrate faith in his handiwork. As shipwrights knocked out the last chocks, the craft slid into the debris and small ice floes of the East River displaying "not the slightest intention of sinking," according to the reporter from the New York *World*. A small, shivering group of onlookers clapped. Among them were a few gamblers who had offered odds on her going under.

Final fitting out now commenced while her crew of fifty-eight awaited the *Monitor*'s commissioning. Ericsson himself had dipped into his savings to add homey niceties to the quarters for the eight officers: tapestry rugs and goat's hair mats, black walnut chests of drawers to match the decor of the berths, lace and damask curtains (though there were no portholes), and carpeted campstools. Candles would be their only illumination, although an oil lamp lit the wardroom. And here in officers' country they would eat from china embossed with the gilt letters, "*Monitor*." This artistic touch, too, was traceable to the Swedish inventor.

Her commanding officer had already been chosen: forty-four-year-old Lieutenant John L. Worden, whose career had been quite undistinguished. But this lean, solemn, polite officer with a long gray beard was lucky. He had been transferred off the sloop USS *Levant* just before she sailed from Honolulu in December 1860—to oblivion. Not a trace of the ship or her crew of almost 200 was ever found. (However, she would be immortalized by Edward Everett Hale's "The Man Without a Country." He chose the *Levant* as more or less the purgatory for Philip Nolan, the hapless, self-proclaimed expatriot.)

Worden had also briefly been a prisoner of war, when taken off a train in Montgomery, Alabama, on April 13, 1861, while en route to a new assignment. Ericsson, however, was not wholly pleased with the Navy's choice to skipper his creation, questioning Worden's "health and energy," and whether he was the "right sort." The Navy Department obviously thought he was.

About two weeks after the *Monitor* was afloat, the *Merrimack* was launched, without ceremony, sometime between February 14 and 17. Only "four marines and a corporal" were on board, according to William R. Cline, one of her crewmen. He added: "There were no invitations to governors and other distinguished men, no sponsor, no bottles of wine, no brass band, no steam whistles, no great crowds . . . "

To command this floating blockhouse, christened "CSS *Virginia*," and her crew of some 100 officers and men, Richmond's naval chief Stephen Mallory chose a Navy veteran of nearly half a century, Captain Franklin Buchanan. "Old Buck," erect, white-haired, balding, and notable for his Roman nose, had been the Naval Academy's first superintendent in 1845. Six years later, he was captain of the USS *Susquehanna* in Commodore Matthew Perry's historic expedition to open up Japan to the West.

A Marylander, he had resigned his commission when he thought the Free State would secede. When it became apparent that the federal government had no intention of losing Maryland, Buchanan asked Navy Secretary Gideon Welles to reinstate him. Welles snubbed him. Becoming emotional, "Old Buck" protested that he would be "miserable" out of the Navy. The latter indicated it would be equally miserable with him in it. Soon his hurt turned bitter and he described his erstwhile shipmates as "vile vagabonds." Mallory, who had pushed the conversion of the *Merrimack*, welcomed this rather pathetic old seadog to the Confederate naval ranks. On March 4, the latter hoisted his flag aboard *Merrimack/Virginia*. Excitedly, two days later the naval secretary queried his new commanding officer: "Can the *Virginia* steam to New York and attack and burn the city? She can, I doubt not, pass Old Point safely, and, in good weather and a smooth sea, could doubtless go to New York. Once in the bay, she could shell and burn the city and shipping . . . peace would inevitably follow. Bankers would withdraw their capital from the city . . . " As an alternative, he suggested that perhaps she could plow up the Potomac and attack Washington. Buchanan did not attempt a reply to this fantasy. If he did not already realize it himself, the Norfolk naval architects did: she would have capsized not far beyond Cape Henry, although a sandbar might mercifully have grounded her before then.

That same Tuesday, March 4, the *Monitor*'s commanding officer, Worden, received orders: "When the weather admits, you will proceed with the *Monitor* under your command to Hampton Roads and report to the senior naval officer there." The "graybeard" was Flag Officer Louis M. Goldsborough, a husky 300-pounder who had entered the Navy as a cadet in 1812. He had pioneered, of all things, the wearing of close-cropped hair by his crew. Commander of the North Atlantic Blockading Squadron, Goldsborough flew his flag from the handsome screw frigate USS *Minnesota*.

On Saturday, March 8, as the *Monitor* tossed through rough seas off the Maryland and Virginia coasts, *Merrimack* steamed from her anchorage down the narrow Elizabeth River. Its banks were lined with cheering people. Buchanan entered Hampton Roads, bent on "carnage, havoc and dismay." Accompanying the juggernaut were three consorts, the *Patrick Henry* and the *Jamestown*, both gunboats, and the tug *Teaser*, all units of the James River Squadron. The *Patrick Henry*, at 1,400 tons, was by far the largest and handsomest. She was the converted side-wheeler *Yorktown*, which once had run to New York. The tugs *Raleigh* and *Beaufort* soon joined the little fleet.

About 12:45 P.M. the Confederate warships cleared Sewell's Point, directly across Hampton Roads from Newport News. There was a slight breeze. Skies were almost cloudless. The alarm was out, passed from ship to ship of the Union assemblage anchored in the Roads, and to Fort Monroe, guarding the northern outlet into Chesapeake Bay. *Minnesota*, raising steam, headed south down the Roads to intercept the long-awaited enemy. A sister frigate, USS *Roanoke*, frantically signalled for tugs. Helpless, she was still awaiting a new propeller shaft.

Captain Gershon van Brunt, of the flagship *Minnesota*, was concerned not only for the safety of the *Roanoke* but also for two handsome old sailing frigates anchored off Newport News, the *Cumberland*, 1,726 tons, and the *Congress*, 1,867 tons. Between them they mounted 74 guns of modest bore and carried a combined complement of about 600. The *Congress*, fresh from the South American station, was an exceptional dowager of a vessel, with some of her cabins trimmed in solid mahogany and bird's-eye maple.

In a day when steam had arrived, the two, picturesque with stately, towering masts, neatly furled sails, and cobwebs of rigging, were no less than anachronisms. As if to accent their whisperings of yesterday and another and long-ago war, it was washday aboard the *Cumberland*: "Every line and spar clearly defined against the blue March sky. . . . The rigging was gay with the red, white and blue of sailors' garments hung out to dry," wrote H. Ashton Ramsay, chief engineer of the *Merrimack*.

Almost as unable to defend herself as the *Roanoke*, the *Cumberland* became aware that she would be the first target. General quarters was sounded. The men tumbled to their many stations as the clothes lines were drawn in; washday was over.

Sweeping past the *Congress*, the big ironclad let loose a volley of small grape shot, which took its toll. Her youthful captain, Lieutenant Joseph B. Smith, ordered a broadside in reply. When the smoke had cleared after "a tremendous roar," it was apparent that the cannon balls had rolled off the *Merrimack* "as harmless as marbles." So thought one of the spectators on shore, William E. Rogers, of the 10th New York Regiment.

At 300 yards, the *Merrimack* hurled a broadside of her own. The result was "simply terrible," in the estimation of Dr. Edward Shippen, surgeon of the *Congress*, adding: "Our clean and handsome gundeck was in an instant changed into a slaughter-pen, with lopped-off legs and arms and bleeding, blackened bodies scattered about by the shells."

Lieutenant Smith knew that his command of only a few days was doomed. He ordered topsails and jib set, the anchors slipped, and signaled for the tug *Zouave* to assist the frigate onto a shoal where she could continue the battle just like any fort.

Lieutenant George U. Morris, executive officer of the *Cumberland*, was attempting, without success, much the same maneuver. (His commander, Captain William Radford, happened to be aboard the disabled *Roanoke* as president of a court martial.) He ran out of time. The *Merrimack* was already in close range and firing. The *Cumberland* shot back with those guns that would bear. So near were both ships to the shore that many artillery pieces at Camp Butler opened up on the ironclad.

Then the *Merrimack* smashed so hard into the frigate that she lost her 1,500-pound, 2½-foot ram. Backing off, she was shaken by three broadsides from her victim. But the *Cumberland* was crushed and sinking. Her gundeck, wrote Lieutenant Thomas O. Selfridge, "was covered with the dead and wounded and slippery with blood . . . rammers and sponges, broken and powder-blackened, lay in every direction; the large galley was demolished and its scattered contents added to the general blood-splattered confusion." Many died in sick bay after taking a direct hit.

Buchanan ordered a second ramming. Now, even as some guns continued firing, Morris sang out, "Every man look out for himself!" As the mangled *Cumberland* sank lower and lower, men commenced leaping into the water. Some made it to shore, others were picked up by rowboats, launches, and tugs as they clung to the debris. On the decks of the *Congress,* one seaman would observe: "We saw her give one lurch, and then she went down like a bar of iron, but her flag still flew at her mast head; all was lost except for honor."

Some 121 were perished, about one-third of the *Cumberland's* complement. The *Minnesota,* which had driven hard on a shoal, was unable to help. The *Roanoke* had been towed out of range, under the big guns of Fort Monroe.

Savoring his easy triumph over the anchored *Cumberland,* Buchanan plowed withing 150 yards of the *Congress,* which was not much more a threat than a jack rabbit, and opened fire. Officers fell beside the men they had commanded. They died from grapeshot, from shell fragments, from wood splinters, bolts, and other parts of the frigate torn loose by the smashing broadsides. "Men were being killed and maimed every minute," Dr. Shippen, her surgeon, would recall. "The shells searched the vessel everywhere!" The wardroom was "a scene of perfect ruin and desolation. Clothing, books, glass, china, photographs, chairs, bedding and tables were all mixed in one confused heap." The *Congress*'s captain, Lieutenant Smith, was dead of a shell splinter in his head. A seaman would write, "We stood and worked in blood, smoke, noise and stench . . . we carried the wounded below to the berth deck . . . never was there such murder!"

No wonder that the executive officer, Lieutenant Austin Pendergast, ordered white sheets run up the masts. But this did not stop the battle. Shore batteries and the grounded *Minnesota*, which surely had not surrendered, kept up a hail of fire against the *Merrimack* and her consorts. Riddled, her engines put out of action, the *Patrick Henry* would have been lost had not the *Jamestown* pulled her back into the Roads.

Buchanan was atop the ironclad's housing and wildly waving a carbine in a manner generally foreign to high command. A soldier with the 20th Indiana, on shore, took aim and fired. "Old Buck" fell, seriously wounded in the groin. Furious, he ordered his executive officer, Lieutenant Thomas Catesby ap R. Jones, "Plug hot shot into her and don't leave her until she's afire!" Almost collapsing, he was carried below. It was, to say the least, about as sporting as a firing squad, considering that the *Congress* had already surrendered.

Now, after 5:00 P.M., the shadows were long, and the tide ebbing. Throwing a few parting shells at the *Minnesota* and the sailing frigate *St. Lawrence,* which was also aground near the flagship, the *Merrimack* started back for the Elizabeth River and her base.

This March 8 had become one of the darkest days in U.S. military history—a total of some 250 killed outright, including five on the *Minnesota*, and more than 100 injured—the greatest casualties in any single U.S. naval action. The Confederates acknowledged some 60 casualties in killed and wounded on the iron-clad and her escorts. According to the engineer, Ramsay, the *Merrimack* was not unscathed, suffering loose plates, broken beams, and the loss of her ram prow.

The strain on her already faltering engines would have to be assessed.

As black smoke from the fiercely burning *Congress* billowed skyward, Major General John E. Wool, seventy-eight-year-old commander of the Department of Virginia, bent over his desk in a casemate of Fort Monroe to transmit fearful tidings to the Secretary of War in Washington, Edwin M. Stanton. His message had to be sent on the evening boat *Adelaide* to Baltimore and thence telegraphed to Washington. The final direct cable link across Hampton Roads and the Chesapeake Bay to Cape Charles and thence up the Eastern Shore of Maryland had not quite been completed.

Even as the *Adelaide* paddled northward, there was a new arrival in the Roads—the *Monitor.* The little metal warship was safe after almost foundering en route. The events of the day would, however, not be fully surprising to Worden when he was advised of them while at anchor beside the threatened *Minnesota.* He had seen the telltale puffs of smoke in mid-afternoon when steaming down the shore.

Shortly after 10:00 P.M., the fires finally reached the *Congress*'s magazines. She blew up, and "certainly a grander sight was never seen," wrote Lieutenant Samuel Dana Greene, twenty-two-year-old executive officer of the *Monitor,* "but it went straight to the marrow of our bones. Not a word was said." Brigadier General Joseph K. Mansfield, commanding Camp Butler and Newport News Point, postscripted his own doleful amen that the explosion was followed by "the stillness of death."

Sunday morning, March 9, had dawned clear and warm in Washington. The *Adelaide* docked in Baltimore about 9:30 A.M. Secretary Stanton received General Wool's telegram minutes later and lost no time in hurrying it to the White House.

Soon, the cabinet was summoned, with others in attendance. The hastily called meeting included, in addition to the

President and Stanton, Navy Secretary Welles, Secretary of State William H. Seward, Secretary of the Treasury Salmon P. Chase, Captain John A. Dahlgren, ordnance expert, Brigadier General Montgomery Meigs, quartermaster general of the Army, Major General George B. McClellan, commanding the Army of the Potomac, and, of course, the presidential secretary, John G. Nicolay. It was as potentially combustible a group as ever assembled in the "War Office" of the White House, both acrimonious and mutually contemptuous. The complex crosscurrents of dislike and distrust found their bitter apogee in the continuing, savage donnybrook between Welles and Stanton.

At once, Dahlgren would observe, there ensued "a hasty and promiscuous emission of opinions from every one, without much regard to rank and some inter-talking which rather confused. Meigs looked desponding and was silent. McClellan was concerned about the troops at Newport News. Seward was composed."

"Stanton, unable to control his strong emotion, walked up and down the room like a caged lion," Nicolay would record. "McClellan was dumbfounded and silent. Lincoln was . . . composed but eagerly inquisitive . . . Chase impatient and ready to utter blame; Seward and Welles hopeful, yet without encouraging reasons to justify their hope."

According to the inveterate diarist Welles, Secretary of War Stanton asserted that the *Merrimack* "could lay every city on the coast under contribution, could take Fortress Monroe; McClellan's mistaken purpose to advance by the Peninsula [to Richmond] must be abandoned, and Burnside would inevitably be captured. [Major General Ambrose Burnside was carrying on a successful expedition to open up the strategic Pamlico Sound area.] Likely the first movement of the *Merrimack* would be to come up the Potomac and disperse Congress, destroy the Capitol and public buildings; or she might go to New York and Boston and destroy those cities, or levy from them contributions sufficient to carry on the War."

Stanton "swung his arms, scolded and raved," Welles continued, and even went "repeatedly" to the window, accompanied by Lincoln himself "and looked down the Potomac—the view being uninterrupted for miles—to see if the *Merrimack* was not coming to Washington." Although Welles was surely not an objective witness where Stanton was involved—and the latter wrote no diaries—Nicolay tended to substantiate the Navy Secretary's impressions in noting, "Mr. Stanton closed his list of sinister prophecies by predicting that a shell or a cannon shot from the *Merrimack* would probably land in the Cabinet room before they separated."

Prior to the sometimes hysterical meeting's disbandment, the President directed McClellan, Meigs, and Dahlgren to arrange as fast as they possibly could the blocking of the Potomac. Stanton, taking cue, dictated telegrams to governors of the coastal states north of Washington and mayors of the principal ports warning of the approach of the *Merrimack* and advising them "to prepare," as Nicolay would report, "all possible resources of their own for defense . . . rafts of timber and other obstructions" to be placed at harbor mouths.

General McClellan hurried dispatches to commanding officers of forts from Delaware to Maine, urging that "you at once place your post in the best possible condition for defense. . . ." Commodore Hiram Paulding, at the New York Navy Yard, was asked to charter the 355-foot steamer *Vanderbilt*, fill her bow with timbers for use as a ram, and plate her sides with iron. He was then to send her to Hampton Roads with orders to smash the *Merrimack*, hopefully, like an eggshell. At almost 5,000 tons, she had been the largest steamer in transatlantic service until the arrival of the *Great Eastern*.

This day the Army and Navy blandly usurped the other's prerogatives, and apparently without objection. Certainly, Stanton was front runner. He airily arranged the commandeering of sixteen canal boats and barges, "if necessary, without consent of owner," loading them with stone for towing down river. There they would be scuttled to render the Potomac impassible. "Stanton's navy," Lincoln would ultimately quip. But none this frenetic Sunday morning appeared to appreciate that if the river was barred to the Confederate dinosaur, so would the Union Navy be bottled up north of the sunken barges. How could it give battle?

While Dahlgren thought the channels up the Potomac would accommodate the draft of the *Merrimack,* he had not been informed that the monster consumed at least half an hour in executing a complete turn. Even in her original incarnation, the frigate would have experienced slow and tedious maneuvering around the shoals south of Alexandria, to say nothing of Washington. Marksmen on the banks could have held target practice aiming at the iron-clad's many gunports. Little boys with rocks might have contributed a token of annoyance, like buzzing bees. Dahlgren's own wonderful cannon, as big as 15 inches in diameter, would surely have finished Mallory's overblown creation.

All in all, there was no wonder that Senator William Pitt Fessenden, of Maine, would write, at bedtime: "I confess I was so frightened . . . that I could not eat my dinner."

With the wounded Buchanan removed ashore, Lieutenant Catesby Jones had succeeded to command of the *Merrimack.* A midshipman in 1836, Jones became, as an ordnance expert, one of the few losses to the Confederacy regretted by the Navy Department. He knew the "*Ericsson*" had arrived from the report of one of his pilots. For some reason he did not pass along this intelligence to his other officers, who went to bed believing that the *Minnesota* would be the morning's principal adversary. The ironclad was not in the best condition, as her surgeon, Dinwiddie Phillips reported: "I found all her stanchions, iron railings, boat davits, and light work of every description swept away, her smokestack cut to pieces, two guns without muzzles, and 98 indentations on her plating, showing where heavy solid shot had struck . . . "

Aboard the *Patrick Henry*, which had suffered such a drubbing from the shore and sustained at least five fatalities, Lieutenant James H. Rochelle had been studying the *Minnesota* through his long glass. He blinked as he observed beside her "such a craft as the eyes of a seaman never looked upon before—an immense shingle floating on the water, with a gigantic cheese box rising from its center; no sails, no wheels, no smokestack, no guns. What could it be?"

Bill Rogers, of the 19th New York at Fort Monroe, came to much the same conclusion. The *Monitor* was "a queer looking little craft which seemed to be neither ship nor anything resembling a ship—something which the soldiers quickly dubbed 'cheese box on a raft.'" Whatever, she seemed "doomed to destruction like her companions. . . . "

The correspondent for the Baltimore *American*, atop the ramparts of the same fort, simply sniffed that the latest naval arrival was " the reverse of formidable."

As crewmen of the *Minnesota*, yet hard aground, tossed into waiting boats or the water all manner of cargo from furniture to provisions in the hopes of lightening her, Worden again reassured Goldsborough and Captain Van Brunt that he would stand by the flagship. Some thought the latter evinced bad manners by observing that he did not think the *Monitor* would be able to help him at all. Indeed, he voiced the opinion of the majority at or around Fort Monroe, certainly seconded by Frederick Curtis, former gunner of the *Congress*: "We did not have much faith in the *Monitor*; we all expected to see the *Merrimack* destroy her."

Sunday morning at Hampton Roads was warm and springlike as it was in Washington. The sun, which "looked red and angry as he rose," according to Colonel LeGrand Bouton Cannon, aide to General Wool, soon gave way to a "singular transparency of the atmosphere."

Shorty before 8:00 A.M., the *Merrimack* arrived within range of the *Minnesota* and let loose a shell which crashed into the flagship's side. Van Brunt, who had signaled, quite unnecessarily, to the *Monitor*, "Attack the enemy!", nonetheless watched with "astonishment" as the little warship "laid herself right alongside of the *Merrimack* and the contrast was that of a pigmy to a giant." Her appearance from around the far side of the *Minnesota* came as quite a surprise to most on the *Merrimack*, looking to Ramsay, the engineering officer, like "a barrelhead afloat with a cheesebox on top of it [that] boldly confronted us."

The methodical Worden maneuvered towards the *Merrimack*'s starboard bow, "on a course nearly at right angles with her line of keel, saving my fire until near enough that every shot might take effect." Within about one-third mile, Worden opened up. James Stephens, of Company K, 20th Indiana, thought from his vantage point at Newport News that this "maiden shot" had struck the foe "plump on the waterline . . . it aroused the fury of the *Merrimack*. She turned and belched an angry volume of fire and shot upon her little rival as though she would blow her out of the water at once."

It was a "rattling broadside," in the judgment of Greene, the *Monitor*'s "exec," the turret and other parts of the ship "were heavily struck, but the shots did not penetrate; the tower was intact, and it continued to revolve. A look of confidence passed over the men's faces." Van Brunt, whose flagship guns were maintaining an almost "constant sheet of flame," was belatedly manifesting respect, as he would later write, "The rebel was pouring broadside after broadside, but almost all her shot flew over the little submerged propeller, and when they struck the bombproof tower the shot glanced off without producing any effect."

Jones, acting captain of the *Merrimack*, noted in frustration, "She and her turret appeared to be under perfect control. Her light draft enabled her to move about us at pleasure.

She once took position for a short time where we could not bring a gun to bear on her." Ramsay, the *Merrimack*'s engineering officer, recorded, "We hovered about each other in spirals, gradually contracting the circuits until we were within point-blank range, but our shell glanced from the *Monitor*'s turret just as hers did from our sloping sides . . . The cannonade continued without perceptible damage to either of the combatants."

Bill Rogers, at Fort Monroe, being reminded of David and Goliath, continued: "Truly this odd little craft was no match for the great monster . . . With breathless suspense we listened to this firing, but could see nothing for the clouds of smoke. We heard the whistle of the shells and the shot, and we could recognize the shots of the *Monitor*. . . . When the thunder ceased, oh! We thought, the 'cheese box' had gone to the bottom. Gradually, the smoke lifted and there lay the two antagonists, backing, filling and jockeying for position, then at it again, and again the cloud of smoke which settled over their struggle hid them from view."

Acting master of the *Monitor* John Webber thought Worden "as cool as a man playing a game of chess." Louis Stodder, another acting master (a now nonexistent naval classification) and also navigating officer, was working the little steam engine that turned the turret. Leaning against the latter when it was struck by a shot, he was stunned and sent below. Alban Stimers, the chief engineer, replaced him. It was difficult not only to start the turret revolving, but to check it once in motion. (Stimers, who had been chief engineer of the old *Merrimack*, served also with Ramsay.) The gunners, stripped to the waist, sweating, worked in smoke and semidark. It required at least eight minutes between rounds.

Now it occurred to Worden that he could break the *Merrimack*'s rudder or propeller by running close to her stern. He tried—and missed by no more than two feet. However, the initial frustration of the latter's acting commander mounted.

"We could only see her guns when they were discharged," Jones found. "We wondered how proper aim could be taken in the very short time the guns were in sight. . . . The *Virginia*, however, was a large target, and generally so near that the *Monitor*'s shots did not often miss. It did not appear to us that our shells had any effect upon the *Monitor*."

Then the *Merrimack* ran hard onto a shoal, two miles away from the *Minnesota*, which continued her tremendous broadsides at the foe. The *Monitor* bore in, rattling "every chink in our armor," by the estimation of Ramsay. Jones signaled the *Patrick Henry* and *Jamestown* for a tow, as the engineers fired the boilers to the bursting point. Reluctantly, the consorts started for the mother ship, knowing full well that the *Monitor* could sink them with one round.

Fortunately for the small wooden ships, the ironclad, after a mighty effort, hauled free. Jones now concluded that, "our fire made no impression on the *Monitor*, [and] we determined to ram her if possible." According to Lieutenant Wood, "nearly an hour" was consumed in endeavoring to steer the *Merrimack* into position. He could but repeat his earlier observations that she was indeed as "unwieldy as Noah's Ark."

Worden, with ample time to observe the enemy's maneuvering, advised the turret: "Look out now, they're going to run us down, give them both guns!" For the *Monitor*'s paymaster, William Keeler, it was "a moment of terrible suspense."

Jones, perhaps belatedly aware that he had lost his ram in crushing the *Cumberland*, ordered reverse engines. Worden shouted to his helmsman, "Hard a-port!"

The *Merrimack* struck only a glancing blow. Ramsay, beside his engines, did not feel "the slightest shock." But the reporter for the Baltimore *American*, through his long glass, watched as the *Monitor* "spun around like a top and, as she got her bearing again, sent one of her formidable missiles into her huge opponent." The collision had caused a leak in the

Confederate's hull, making it necessary to start the pumps. Jones found it "alarming."

Keeler labeled the sounds of the conflict "terrible," not only the concussion of the foe's shells against the turret, but a few strays from the hard-firing *Minnesota* as well. Two men leaning against the turret, as Stodder, were toppled "senseless" and had to be carried below.

The *Merrimack* was experiencing similar casualties. Her armor plate was loosened while, according to Lieutenant Wood, "All the crews of the after guns were knocked over by the concussion and bled from the nose and ears."

Jones called for boarders while the antagonists remained close together. As the first of them prepared to leap onto the low-lying deck, Worden drew off. He had anticipated such an attempt. Ashore, it was noticed that the *Monitor*'s flagstaff was gone – shot off, or a token of surrender? Worries were put to rest as a daring sailor appeared and raised a new flag before scurrying back to safety.

A broadside from the hulking *Merrimack* smashed into the chief engineer's stateroom and other compartments of the *Minnesota*, starting a fire and rupturing the boiler of the nearby tug *Dragon*. The *Monitor* drew nearer to the flagship to serve as a shield. The act of the latter drew praise from Ramsay: "The *Monitor* gallantly rushed to her rescue, passing so close under our submerged stern that she almost snapped off our propeller . . . Lieutenant Wood trained the stern gun on her when she was only 20 yards from its muzzle and delivered a rifle-pointed shell which dislodged the iron logs sheltering the *Monitor*'s conning tower, carrying away the steering-gear and signal apparatus."

While it was not true that navigability was impaired, Worden's eyes were filled with powder, "utterly blinding and in a degree stunning me." Pete Williams, the quartermaster who stood by Worden's side and had seen "right into the bore" of the enemy guns, was miraculously unhurt. Hastily sum-

"There is not now a ship in the English Navy," wrote the *Times* of London, "except for [the *Black Prince* and the *Warrior*] that it would not be madness to trust to an engagement with that little *Monitor*."

It required a month to replace iron plates on the *Merrimack* and otherwise make her seaworthy. Yet both the Confederate ironclad and the *Monitor* were under orders to avoid a repetition of their dramatic encounter. Washington and Richmond alike feared either's destruction or capture.

The "Big Thing," as some in Fort Monroe referred to the *Merrimack*, was given a new commander, Commodore Joseph Tattnall, a grizzled veteran of the War of 1812. But as he and other Confederate naval officers plotted ways by which they might subdue the *Monitor*, time ran out. A federal expedition of less than 6,000 troops recaptured Norfolk on Saturday, May 10. The defenders evacuated the Navy Yard and other installations in haste.

Not forewarned of the precipitate action, Tattnall raised steam in the hopes of going up the James to the defense of Richmond. Coal, ballast, and many supplies were jettisoned to lighten the "Big Thing" so that she could pass Harrison's Bar in the broad river. About midnight, the old commodore realized he could neither cross the bar nor fight his way through the Union fleet coming toward him. This included the *Monitor*, the newly arrived ironclad *Galena*, and other formidable warships. He dropped anchor off Craney Island, at the mouth of the Elizabeth River. As his crew was ferried ashore, a slow fuse was lit which would burn its way to the magazine containing nearly 18 tons of powder.

Aboard the nearing USS *Dacotah*, Lieutenant Samuel Franklin, her executive officer, observed the progress of the fire aboard the *Merrimack* to its crescendo: "The casemate grew hotter and hotter, until finally it became red-hot, so that we could distinctly mark its outlines, and remained in this condition for fully half an hour, when, with a tremendous explosion, the *Merrimack* went into the air and was seen no more."

It was the fiery end of a mere eight weeks of operational life. The "iron diadem of the South," as some knew her, was gone.

The *Monitor* spent a part of the summer of 1862 helping to cover McClellan's ill-fated peninsular campaign. She languished in Hampton Roads most of November and December until receiving orders to Beaufort, North Carolina, probably to serve in the blockade of Wilmington, favorite port of the cargo runners.

Luck ran out for the *Monitor.* In tow from the broad-beamed sidewheeler USS *Rhode Island*, she foundered in a gale off Hatteras in the early hours of December 31, 1862 and took with her sixteen officers and men. But her short life had scarcely been in vain. Even the least visionary could appreciate that the little iron vessel had dramatically altered the fashions in warships and, in so doing, rewritten the books on naval operations.

Seventy-one *Monitor*-class ironclads would be ordered during the remainder of the century, and fifty actually commissioned. They evolved into ocean-crossing, double-turreted warships of 6,000 tons, 100 feet longer than the first *Monitor*, topped with a bridge, mast, and superstructure. The British, however, would herald the next century's battleships or "armored cruisers" when naval engineers launched the *Devastation* in 1873. She was a twin-turreted prototype with a single mast.

Now, certainly the world's wooden-hulled men o' war were relegated to virtual museum pieces. The U.S. Navy's beautiful steam frigates including the *Hartford, Pensacola,* and *Minnesota* became training or receiving ships at naval yards, or memorials beside the parks of port cities. There, children could play atop the long cold guns, and shriek with disappointment as mothers hauled them off the rigging. The wonderful old vessels were as immobile and innocuous as the statuary springing up in village greens from Maine to Georgia, immortalizing both "Billy Yank" and "Johnny Reb."

The "steel navies" that would shake the balance of power and help reshape world history came fully into being during the 1880s. In 1883, the U.S. Congress appropriated $1.3 million—then a great sum—to start construction on three "protected cruisers," the *Atlanta* and *Boston* and, the largest, the *Chicago*, at 4,500 tons. Mounted in her main turrets were 8- and 6-inch breech-loading guns. While the *Chicago* could boast twin propellers, they nonetheless were driven by old-fashioned reciprocating engines. And, as if the designers weren't fully comfortable with this machinery, they added sail rigging, like vestigial tails in the evolutionary process. The masts, however, eventually had to go. And they did in blueprints in 1885 for the slightly larger cruisers, the *Charleston* and the *Newark*. A year later, the "second class battleships" *Texas* and *Maine*, 6,000 tons plus, became more than a gleam in the shipbuilders' eyes.

Finally convinced, Congress accelerated the program with the Naval Act of 1890 which would produce the *Indiana*, *Massachusetts* and *Oregon*, of 10,228 tons. Five more were appropriated for in 1895 and 1896—the *Kearsarge* class, which included the *Kentucky*. The 11,500-tonners mounted 13-inch batteries.

The U.S. Navy rose to fifth place among the world's fighting fleets. More than that, with the Spanish-American War in 1898, her brand new sea force propelled the United States into the status of an empire. The conflict had been precipitated by the sinking of the USS *Maine* the night of February 15 in Havana harbor, with 260 casualties. The battleship had been dispatched to Cuba to protect American lives during a period of turmoil.

The obsolete Spanish fleets were easily outgunned in Cuba and in the Philippines. The naval battles both in Manila Bay and Santiago, Cuba, revealed a surprise to the ordnance people concerning guns and gunnery. "Someone made a compilation," wrote Captain Edward Beach, a present-day historian and novelist, "which purported to prove that of several thousand shells fired . . . in these two sea fights, less than 300 had actually hit anything; another calculation was that none of the great 13-inch projectiles—and only 42 of 8-inch or larger—fired off Santiago struck their targets."

Whatever the merits, or lack of them, of the conflict, whether the Spanish had actually destroyed the battleship *Maine* or the blast had been accidental, the United States would and could not return to yesterday (though in some ways she tried, for another fifteen years or so).

The lessons of Santiago Bay and Manila Bay were not lost upon the Japanese. Seven years later, on May 27, 1905, Tokyo's capital ships annihilated the Russian navy in the Battle of Tsushima Strait. Although their major warships were even numerically (with twelve on each side) the Czar's sea arm had failed to modernize. Some Russian guns, in fact, were muzzle loaders. Port Arthur, now without a primary line of defense, fell to the conqueror. Thus, this first clash of iron ships was a decisive factor in the Russo-Japanese War. As a result, Japan would be the dominant Asian power for nearly half a century.

In 1906, Great Britain launched the first real battleship, HMS *Dreadnought*, whose very name would become synonymous with the largest of warships. This prototype displaced almost 18,000 tons and was powered, as another first, by steam turbines which made possible a speed of 21 knots. Twin 12-inch guns were mounted in five fully self-contained turrets.

The United States possessed nothing to remotely compare with *Dreadnought*. President Teddy Roosevelt, nonetheless, did not want his navy forgotten. He ordered sixteen battleships, some of them approaching obsolescence, painted glaring white and dispatched them on a 'round-the-world cruise in December 1907. The USS *Connecticut* was designated flagship of this the Great White Fleet.

Her naval architects, however, were bending over their drafting boards, knowing that the Great Powers—Germany, Japan, and France, in addition to the United Kingdom—were already fashioning navies that would make units of the White Fleet look like bathtub toys, and just about as menacing. Between the return of the showy white fleet and 1917, the United States would float the 26,000-ton *Arkansas*, carrying a main battery of 12-inch guns; the *New York*, 27,000 tons; *Nevada*, 29,000 tons; *Arizona*, 31,400 tons, and *Pennsylvania* and the *New Mexico*, both 33,000 tons. These last five were all armed with 14-inch guns.

Britain kept pace with such as the mighty battle cruiser *Queen Elizabeth*, 31,000 tons, and with a main battery of 15-inchers; Germany with the *Bayern*, 28,000 tons, also with 15-inch guns; France, the *Provence*, 23,000 tons, with 13-inch guns; Italy, the *Conte di Cavour*, 24,000 tons, with 12.6-inch guns; and Japan, the *Fuso*, 35,000 tons, with 14-inch guns.

This vast international assemblage of juggernauts, steel-plated sea monsters of incredible destruction, would end up in the Great War at sea as if this really were the only way to satisfactorily prove their worth.

The mightiest test by far would come at Jutland in June 1916 when England's Home Fleet clashed head-on with the Kaiser's High Seas Fleet.

Britain came out badly, losing fourteen warships aggregating 114,000 tons, almost double the casualties of the High Seas Fleet. Their total of 6,000 dead was about twice that of the German foe. The giant battle cruisers, *Queen Mary, Invincible,* and *Inflexible* were blown to pieces, with only twenty-four survivors out of some 4,000 aboard the three. This tragedy beyond measure would evoke the historic understatement of Admiral David Beatty, commanding the battle cruisers: "There seems to be something wrong with our bloody ships today." (The admiral was quite correct insofar as the battle cruisers were concerned. Inadequate flash protection allowed the explosion of hits above deck to travel all the way down to the magazines, as if following a powder train.) "Glorious End of Our Cruisers," as one London paper headlined, it was not.

One could well ask, what was the meaning of this epic encounter of giant, turreted warships? Foremost, perhaps, that stalemate would prevail when major powers possessed equally matched forces. Cynically enough, Hanson Baldwin, the late military analyst and historian, alluded to "Admiral Death" as the only undisputed victor.

There would never be another Jutland. Yet the era of the fleet "heavies" was far from over, despite the dramatic emergence of the aircraft carrier. The "battlewagons" simply grew bigger. By the time of World War II they included the USS *Iowa*, 46,000 tons, mounting 16-inch guns; HMS *King George* V, 38,000 tons, with 14-inch guns; Nazi Germany's *Bismarck*, 42,000 tons, with 15-inch guns; France's *Richelieu*, 39,000 tons, with 15-inch guns; Italy's *Littorio*, 41,000 tons, with 15-inch guns; and Japan's stunning *Yamato*, 65,000 tons, with a main battery of 18.1-inch cannon. (Thereby, her displacement was nearly 70 times that of the USS *Monitor*.)

Some five battleship-to-battleship duels were recorded in World War II. On May 24, 1941, the *Bismarck*, Hitler's mightiest man o' war, sank HMS *Hood*, 41,000 tons, in the North Atlantic. Just three out of a complement of 1,416 survived, underscoring anew the vulnerabilities of the old battle cruisers.

Through a combination of aerial reconnaissance and the interception of enemy naval messages (the British had compromised the German Enigma machine ciphers in a top secret operaton coded "Ultra") the *Bismarck* was located two days later 700 miles west of Brest, racing for refuge. A Royal Navy force, led by the battleships HMS *Rodney*, *King George* V, and *Prince of Wales*, including as well two carriers and cruisers, pounded the pride of the Nazi fleet to pieces. The

Bismarck went down on May 27 without surrendering, carrying with her all but 110 of her large crew of 2,300.

The previous year, on July 3, 1940, in Mers-el Kebir harbor near Oran, Algeria, the new Vichy French battleship *Bretagne* was destroyed, and the *Provence* and *Dunkerque* seriously damaged by attacking Royal Navy battleships. Churchill would recall that the decision to keep the warships out of German control was one of his hardest and saddest of the war. Admiral Andrew Cunningham, commanding Britain's Mediterranean fleet, had given the French only a few hours in which to steam to sea or scuttle the ships. The inevitable heavy loss of French lives drove a further wedge between Vichy France and Great Britain sparking a hatred that would continue even after the war.

A week later, the Italian flagship *Giulio Cesare,* off the coast of Calabria at the Italian "boot," was hit squarely by a shell from HMS *Warspite* at a range of 15 miles. This record for a shell actually reaching its target has not been exceeded, although battleships' 15- and 16-inch guns are supposed to have a range of more than 25 miles.

Devastating as was the action of the Royal Navy's big ships in the Mediterranean, it was not the classic dueling that took place elsewhere.

The 32,000-ton *Scharnhorst* remained a threat to merchant shipping and especially to the perilous Murmansk route. Searching, on December 26, 1943, for a large convoy passing Norway the *Scharnhorst* instead was met by HMS *Duke of York.* After a furious gun duel, the British battleship sank her adversary. Only 26 out of her crew of 2,000 were saved.

In mid-November 1942, the U.S. battleships *Washington* and *South Dakota* fought the Japanese *Kirishima* and her escorting cruisers and destroyers off Guadalcanal. Crippled and vulnerable from an electrical malfunction, the *South Dakota,* hit repeatedly, dropped out of the engagement. Several broadsides from the *Washington* sent the *Kirishima* to the bottom.

PT boats accounted for the battleship *Fuso* in the confused melee of Leyte Gulf, October 25–26, 1944. Spread out over almost 500,000 square miles of the Philippine Archipelago, the battle has been described as the greatest sea fight in history, certainly with respect to the number of ships involved. Severely damaged in the engagement (which involved as well aircraft and various classes of warships), another battleship, the *Yamashiro*, was given the coup de grace by several old-class U.S. battleships which had been hit at Pearl Harbor, then repaired and modernized. Thus, there is a question whether *Yamashiro*'s loss could be altogether attributed to a "battleship duel."

The huge pagoda-like *Yamato*—her monster guns virtually unused—fell victim the following May 1945, not to other surface craft, but to waves of U.S. Navy bombers. The Allies proved thereby that they had learned a bitter lesson from the sinking of HMS *Prince of Wales* and the *Repulse* December 10, 1941, by Japanese planes off Malaya. By chance, Cecil Brown, the CBS correspondent, was on board the *Repulse*. He wrote a dramatic account of the disaster in his memoirs, *From Suez to Singapore*.

In the closing months of the Pacific War, American and British battleships steamed almost unchallenged up and down Nippon's home islands, bombarding coastal targets. This day-and-night punishment played a powerful role in the weakening of the enemy's will to resist. In fact, some cited this sea-to-land action plus incendiary air raids as further evidence that the foe would have surrendered without resort to the atom bomb.

Seemingly, rockets, cruise missiles, and certainly aircraft have rendered the ponderous battleships obsolete. Yet a few, refitted, fly the commission pennant of the U.S. Navy. Two, the *Missouri* and the *Wisconsin*, served in the Persian Gulf, with the added capabilities of long-range missile launchers.

Whatever else may lie in their future, the fleet "heavies" have endured for well over a century. The concept was born in the little *Monitor.* Not even Ericsson could have foreseen such a destiny.

Chapter Four

RMS *Lusitania*

America before 1914 was the land of Pollyanna and Peter Pan, the literature of Harold Bell Wright and Kathleen Norris, the "Hesitation Waltz" and "The Beautiful Ohio," of country fairs and lawn parties at Newport, moonlit rides in a Stutz Bearcat, or holding hands in the back seat of the last trolley from the amusement park, while the Europe of travel posters was the sound of Big Ben, the Tuileries gardens of Paris in the spring, and the splendor of Rhine castles. Then came August 14, 1915, 1916, 1917 . . . nothing anywhere would be the same—ever. For Alice in Wonderland had gone to war. It was the end of innocence.

On a raw, wet morning, April 2, 1917, the Monday after Palm Sunday, a solemn President Wilson stood before a joint session of Congress to deliver the most grave request of his administrations.

Not a sound disturbed the almost oppressive silence as legislators leaned forward in their seats to catch the least intonation as the former president of Princeton spoke in professorial tones. Then, raising his voice, the man "who kept us out of war" declared, "We shall not choose the path of submission!"

The entire chamber was on its feet, clapping and cheering, led by a Confederate veteran, Chief Justice Edward White. Now, applause, shouts, and other spontaneous utterances greeted nearly every statement of the Chief Executive: "The recent course of the Imperial Government . . . [is] nothing less than war against the Government and people of the United States . . . we have no quarrel with the German people . . . we are now about to accept gage of battle with this natural foe of Liberty . . . the world must be made safe for democracy . . . the right is more precious than peace, and we shall fight for the things which we have always carried nearest our hearts."

Woodrow Wilson had required just thirty-six minutes to ask that Congress "formally accept the status of belligerent which has thus been thrust upon us." It was easily the most fateful moment in American history since Lincoln's call for volunteers or his Emancipation Proclamation. But its genesis, its impelling causes had not just happened, not in the past few days, weeks, or even months. To discover them one must look further back in time, to 1907.

Just eighteen years after the tug *Stormcock* had towed the *Great Eastern* to the shipbreakers, the largest steamship since Brunel's creation quit John Brown's yard in Clydebank, Scotland, and made ready for her maiden voyage. The year was 1907, six years after King Edward VII finally succeeded Victoria to the throne of England and only three years before death would end his brief reign and three years before the appearance of Halley's Comet.

Massiveness alone—32,000 tons displacement—did not make RMS (Royal Mail Ship) *Lusitania* the greatest steamship afloat in those early years of the century. Her speed, engines, luxury, and many innovations all added up to the first of the century's superliners. None could foresee the Pandora's box in her destiny.

Lusitania's 790-foot length and 87-foot beam—a better than 9–1 ratio—resulted in a slim-waisted hull more like that of a cruiser or one of the old clipper ships than a passenger liner. Her slender lines guaranteed as well a sickening high-speed roll. Four steam turbines, producing 70,000 horsepower, drove four huge propellers to make possible speeds up to 30 knots. For the first time she cut the Atlantic crossing time to four and a half days, thus winning the coveted, though physically nonexistent blue Riband. (Turbines for ships had been introduced two years earlier, in 1905, with the appearance of a smaller Cunarder, the *Carmania*, of 19,524 tons.)

Lusitania's luxuries included elevators, cabin telephones, hot and cold running water, and even individual bathrooms. The ship boasted electrification throughout, forced air ventilation, roof gardens splendid with potted palms, a nursery plus diet kitchen for the babies, and a gymnasium.

The Louis VI first-class dining saloon, with its high-domed balcony section, was decorated in white and gold and seated 500. Paintings of the nine muses, modified Corinthian columns, and an immense mahogany sideboard completed the aura of dignified opulence. (Third-class passengers had to be content with simple Doric columns in their eating area.) Overstuffed brocade sofas and lounge chairs interspersed with buttoned grandmother chairs and graceful mahogany tables offered mansion-like comfort in the late-Georgian first-class lounge. Fireplaces proved the ultimate in shipboard comfort.

A hospital satisfied the medical demands of its passengers with at least one doctor and several nurses in attendance. Of course, accommodations were provided for maids and valets, not to mention the ubiquitous nanny. There were kennels and cages for those passengers who could not leave Fido, pussy cat, or whatever at home. Never had the transatlantic voyager, human or otherwise, been so pampered. One more bonus—with a double bottom, even as the *Great Eastern*, and 175 watertight compartments—*Lusitania's* builders felt confident that their tour de force was "unsinkable."

Lusitania was soon joined by an identical companion, *Mauretania*. The "lovely sisters" as the pair were dubbed, inspired a succession of larger and larger superliners in the next half dozen years. They included the 47,000-ton *Aquitania*, the White Star *Olympic*, of comparable size, and her magnificent but ill-fated sister, *Titanic*, of more than 50,000 tons. The Hamburg-American *Vaterland* topped them all; at 58,000 tons she was the largest liner afloat.

By August 1914, *Lusitania* had completed about 100 round-trip crossings and carried almost one-third million passengers. With her sister ship "*Maury*," "*Lusy*" was able to provide weekly service from New York. They were fast, dependable, and very popular.

With the coming of war both Cunard and White Star were faced with the decision: What to do with their liners? *Mauretania* was withdrawn from transatlantic service to be readied as a transport or hospital ship, as was *Aquitania*. The "sisters" flew the blue ensign denoting them as naval auxiliaries (as contrasted with the white ensign of the battle fleet, or familiar "red duster," the merchant flag). Despite this, the *Lusitania* remained on the New York-Liverpool run, advertised as the "Fastest and Largest Steamer now in Atlantic Service."

Part of the rationale was the conviction that Kaiser Wilhelm II would not allow his U-boat captains to attack a passenger vessel carrying women and children. In any case, it was thought that the big Cunarder could outrun a submarine. As she traversed the North Atlantic, through the autumn, winter, and early spring of 1915, the official reasoning seemed to be fully borne out.

Thus on May 1, 1915, *Lusitania* cast off from her familiar Pier 54 on the Hudson River at the foot of 11th Street, for what should have been just another routine sailing. On board were 1,257 passengers, including 159 Americans and 129 children as well as the crew of 702. However, on this Saturday morning a notice appeared in the New York papers, inserted by the Imperial German Embassy in Washington. It read:

> Travellers intending to embark on the Atlantic voyage are reminded that a state of war exists between Germany and her allies and Great Britain and her allies; that the zone of war includes the waters adjacent to the British Isles; that, in accordance with formal notice given by the Imperial German Government, vessels flying the flag of Great Britain or of any of her allies are liable to destruction in those waters and that travelers sailing in the war zone on ships of Great Britain or her allies do so at their own risk.

The New York *World* had placed the notice, perhaps by chance, next to Cunard's announcement of sailings of the *Lusitania* as well as smaller ships. It was surmounted by a sketch of the superliner. Because of the somber warning, the impending departure had attracted many reporters, photographers, and even newsreel cameramen. The representative of one paper caught the ship's captain, William Turner, a veteran salt whose career went back to sailing ships, on the promenade deck of the great liner. A relief captain this crossing (for the ailing "Paddy" Dow), he now stood next to a frequent and notable passenger, Alfred Gwynne Vanderbilt, at thirty-eight one of the world's wealthiest men, who was en route to London to inspect his stables.

When questioned, Turner laughed and remarked, "It's the best joke I've heard in many days, this talk of torpedoing! Do you think all these people would be booking passage . . . if they thought this ship could be caught by a German submarine? Well, I've never heard of one that could make 27 knots." He was joined in mirth by the millionaire playboy. Vanderbilt had displayed the same nonchalance when queried in 1912 about the cancellation of his booking the night before the *Titanic* sailed. It was the same indifference that some of his circle found often annoying.

Either Turner was kidding his celebrated shipmate, or he himself did not know the facts. This voyage, six of *Lusy*'s twenty-five boilers would be cold in order to save coal, meaning that only 144 of her 192 furnaces could be fired. She would be lucky to clock 20 knots.

As in any sailing of a great liner, there was the usual quota of notables like Vanderbilt aboard the *Lusitania.* Among the better known was Elbert Hubbard, author of *A Message to Garcia* and other popular little essays. The long-haired, affable eccentric called the "Sage of East Aurora" was also the founder of the Roycrofters community of craftsmen in that upstate New York town. The well-known producer Charles Frohman was traveling with actress Rita Jolivet, her brother-in-law George Vernon, and author/playwright Justus Forman. This was an annual visit to London for the producer, but it was clouded by his knowledge that the great actress Ellen Terry, as well as the Isadora Duncan dancers, had transferred to the *New York* because of the submarine threat. Lady Mackworth, daughter of British industrialist D. A. Thomas and a militant suffragette who had been jailed several times for her activities, was not so easily deterred. Nor was Madame Marie Depage, wife of the famous Belgian surgeon and hospital director, Dr. Antoine Depage. She was returning from a lecture tour in the United States on behalf of Belgian relief.

Perhaps less well known but equally influential in their fields were: Theodate Pope, architect and spiritualist from Connecticut, who was en route for a psychical meeting in London to join Sir Oliver Lodge and Conan Doyle among others; Paul Crompton of Philadelphia, a director of the Booth Steamship Company Ltd. returning to England with his wife, four sons and two daughters ranging in age from nine months to seventeen years, as well as the childrens' governess, Dorothy Allen; Albert L. Hopkins, president of the Newport News Shipbuilding and Drydock Co.; Oliver P. Bernard, scenic director of the Boston Opera House and Covent Garden, London; Charles A. Plamondon of Chicago, president of a large machinery manufacturing company; and Allen D. Loney, New

York and London socialite who had been driving for the Red Cross in France, now returning with his wife and fourteen-year-old daughter, Virginia Bruce.

And then there were the hundreds of other passengers, "little people" known only to family, friends, and neighbors. A random sampling might include Elizabeth Duckworth of Taftville, Connecticut, going to work in the mills of her native Blackburn, England; George Kessler, New York wine merchant; Dorothy Conner of Medford, Oregon, one of a number of Red Cross volunteers and nurses; James H. "Jay" Brooks of South Paris, Maine, representative of a tire chain company; twelve-year-old Avis Dolphin of Ontario, traveling alone to live with her grandparents in England; Rev. H. L. Gwyer, 6-foot-4-inch Episcopal minister from Calgary in western Canada and his bride of three weeks, Margaret; another Canadian, Florence Padley, of Vancouver, five months pregnant, going to Liverpool to stay with friends; Father Basil Maturin, Roman Catholic chaplain at Oxford University; C. T. Hill, a tobacco salesman from Richmond, Virginia; Ogden Hammond, a businessman who called sleepy Bernardsville, New Jersey, home; A. J. Mitchell, a Raleigh Cycle representative from West Bridgford, England; and Charles Lauriat, a Boston bookseller.

Several dozen of the better known passengers including Plamondon and Vanderbilt had been handed telegrams just before boarding. These were personal warnings not to sail on the *Lusitania* as she would be "torpedoed." Some were signed ominously "morte," others simply with a common name such as John Smith. Most recipients agreed these were the product of a crank. Others, like Elbert Hubbard, while making light of the possibility, did not discount it entirely. He had recently completed one of his little essays titled "Who Lifted the Lid off Hell?" which did not accord encomiums to Kaiser Wilhelm. He entertained few illusions as to the lengths that the monarch might go to have the last word.

The Cunarder was an RMS vessel, an international postman

for the Royal Mail. She was a carrier of people, not a freighter. Thus her cargo capacity was minimal, accenting food items for a hungry British Isles. On board were 342,000 pounds of beef, 217 pounds of cheese, 185,000 pounds of bacon, 205 barrels of Connecticut oysters, and lesser quantities of lard, beans, pork, and biscuits.

The *Lusitania* had also been loaded with 4,200 cases of small-caliber (practice) rifle ammunition from the Remington Arms Co., 1,250 cases of empty shrapnel shells, 200,000 pounds of sheet brass, machine parts, and an assortment of shoelaces, leaf tobacco, drugs, dental and other goods. The total cargo value was manifested with the Collector of Customs at a modest $750,000. It was an average and unnoteworthy volume for the *Lusitania.* Not on the manifest were an undisclosed number of mail bags and a rumored $6 million in gold bullion.

Aided by three tugs, the liner backed from her pier at 12:30 P.M. She had been delayed two and a half hours by a routine wartime search for explosive devices and for transferring passengers from the *Cameronia,* which had just been called to the colors by the Royal Navy. Newsreels plainly revealed Captain Turner on a bridge wing, while Elbert Hubbard was distinct from other passengers on the boat deck because of his floppy hat and enormous bow tie. "Fra Elbertus," as he was sometimes called, stood with his second wife, Alice, waving. Reporters would remember that he had joked with them about his recent essay, wondering if "Kaiser Bill" might try to get even with him for its unflattering remarks. Alice saw no humor whatsoever in the subject.

Even as *Lusitania* steamed down Ambrose Channel, the United States-flag tanker *Gulflight* was torpedoed without warning by the U-30 off the Scilly Islands in the English Channel. Although the vessel was beached, three American lives were lost including that of her captain, who succumbed to a heart attack.

If this was a stupid Teutonic act against a neutral vessel plainly marked, the Germans had the capability to do so. With at least six submarines operating around the British Isles, the Kaiser's underwater fleet was fast building up—about thirty had been launched since the commencement of hostilities, supplementing the twenty-eight already in commission and on the prowl. The principal target was, of course, Britain's jugular—the maritime lifeline of food and supplies without which she could not continue the struggle.

Two days out of Emden, making its first landfall (lonely Fair Island between the Shetlands and Orkneys) was U-20, en route to relieve U-24 and U-32. Youthful Kapitanleutnant Walther Schwieger, blue-eyed and rather baby-faced, had received very general orders for this cruise:

> Large English troop transports expected starting from Liverpool, Bristol, Dartmouth . . . get to stations on the fastest possible route around Scotland; hold them as long as supplies permit . . . submarines are to attack transport ships, merchant ships, warships.

Aboard this time was Helmsman Lanz a pilot, not a regular member of a U-boat crew, who "knows all English ships by their build and can tell at once at what speed they generally run."

Hunting had been good in late April and early May—several trawlers, small freighters, and colliers had been sunk by U-boats between Scotland and the Scillies. On Wednesday, May 5, Schwieger arrived on station off the Old Head of Kinsale, a prominent Irish headland about 15 miles west of Cobh, or Queenstown. He at once sank the schooner *Earl of Latham,* carrying a cargo of Irish bacon, eggs and potatoes for Liverpool. The major port was scarcely 270 miles to the northeast, on the Mersey beside the Irish Sea. The crew climbed into the lifeboats with no time to spare.

The same evening Schwieger fired a torpedo at a 3,900-ton Norwegian steamer, missed, and crash-dived when it appeared his intended victim was about to ram. The next day, Thursday, May 6, Schwieger torpedoed two 6,000-ton Harrison liners, the *Candidate* and *Centurion*—without warning—off Waterford, on the south coast of Ireland. The site of the attack was east of Queenstown near the Coningbeg lightship and the entrance to St. George's Channel into the Irish Sea. All aboard both steamers made it into the lifeboats. "Since the fog does not abate," Schwieger logged, "I now resolve upon the return journey." He reversed course and headed back toward Kinsale.

Meanwhile, the *Lusitania*'s voyage had been typical of the North Atlantic in mid-spring: mostly calm, misty, with a good swell off the Grand Banks. Patches of fog triggered throaty blasts from the liner's big horn. To young Dorothy Conner it had been "a dull, dreary, stupid trip." This uneventfulness was, of course, welcomed by the captain and his mates. Not until midweek did the clouds lift, boosting morale. Charles Plamondon, a diarist, wrote, "Pleasant weather, sunshine all day."

On Thursday evening, at 8:30, as survivors from the Harrison liners were struggling ashore, Marconi, or radio operator Stewart Hutchinson aboard the *Lusitania* copied from the British Admiralty: "Submarines active off south coast of Ireland." Half an hour later, the Admiralty transmitted from its powerful towers on Valentia Island on the southwest coast of Ireland: "To all British ships 0005 (Greenwich): "Take Liverpool pilot at bar and avoid headlands. Pass harbors at full speed. Steer mid-channel course. Submarines off Fastnet."

Captain Bill Turner, however, would later testify that he was confused as to what was meant by "mid-channel." The figure of 140 miles as the total width of a channel somehow came to mind. In any case, although he was nearing Fastnet Rock, a prominent navigation point off the southwest tip of Ireland, the captain did not change course. He felt he had already taken necessary precautions. Lifeboats had been swung out. Many of the watertight bulkheads had been closed. Steam pressure was nearly maximum: 195 pounds per square inch. The liner was making 21 knots, though the cold furnaces had not been fired up.

During Thursday night the same "0005" warning message was repeated at intervals, seven times altogether. Nothing was mentioned, however, of the U-20's three torpedoings, much less the ominous fact that a total of twenty-three merchantmen had been sunk off the British Isles since the *Lusitania's* sailing from New York. This attrition should not have been altogether surprising since there wasn't much to control the U-boats except the second-rate Irish Coast Patrol. Rear Admiral H. L. A. Hood flew his flag from the twenty-year-old 5,000-ton cruiser *Juno*. The rest of his squadron consisted of three other equally obsolete cruisers, some overage destroyers and a potpourri of armed yachts and trawlers capable only of inadequate speeds when they could run at all.

However, the Admiralty was not deliberately neglecting this "lifeline of empire." The Royal Navy's best units were at the Dardanelles, supporting the disastrous Gallipoli campaign, and guarding the east coast against the Kaiser's powerful High Seas Fleet across the North Sea.

Friday, May 7, dawned foggy. It was so thick that Turner slowed the *Lusitania* down to 15 knots. The marked reduction of speed was both obvious and disquieting to the passengers. "You could hear whenever you passed a group of passengers," noted Michael Byrne, of New York, "'Well why are we not making full speed of 25 knots? As Captain Turner told us at our concert, we could run away from any submarine.'" Mrs. Theodore Naish, of Kansas City, "thought we could row a boat faster than we were moving." She and her fellow passengers were upset anyhow by the intermittent, penetrating sound of the horn. Wouldn't it also give away their position to U-boats? Byrne was additionally disturbed because he had prowled the great liner looking for armament. When he found none he concluded the ship was "defenceless."

Turner guessed in mid-morning that he had passed Fastnet Rock, somewhere off the port beam in the swirling mists. Finally, a few minutes after 11:00 A.M., the fog dispersed to reveal a clear, warm day and flat seas. There was only a moderate ground swell from the Irish coast. The captain ordered speed increased to 18 knots. Twenty-five minutes later, another message was received from the admiralty: "Submarine active in southern part of Irish Channel, last heard of 20 miles south of Coningbeg Light Vessel. Make certain *Lusitania* gets this."

In Liverpool, Alfred A. Booth, chairman of the board of Cunard, greatly disturbed by the news of the sinkings of the Harrison ships, had asked that their names be included in the message. For some reason, they were not.

Before noon, a thin haze of land appeared off the port beam. Captain Turner figured it must be Brow Head, a medium-high promontory about 15 miles northwest of Fastnet, almost on the west coast of Ireland. Yet, the *Lusitania* should have already passed Fastnet and been approaching Queenstown. Then, at 12:40 P.M. yet another radio message arrived: "Submarine 5 miles south of Cape Clear, proceeding west when sighted at 10:00 A.M."

Twenty minutes later, a familiar landfall, Galley Head, was recognized. Yet, this promontory was some 40 miles to the east of Brow Head. Surely the liner could not have covered 40 miles from Brow Head in approximately one hour. The earlier landfall, thereby, could not have been Brow Head. If indeed Turner were looking at Galley Head, he believed the submarine off Cape Clear (near Fastnet Rock) must be well astern of the *Lusitania*.

However, as he was to testify, he did not know "with any certainty" where he was—the ultimate nightmare of command. Turner's conclusion was almost a mariner's reflexive action when in doubt: sail close to land for a good look. He altered course by 20 degrees toward the Irish coast.

He came so close by 1:30 P.M., perhaps 12 miles offshore, that passengers excitedly discerned the outlines of trees, rooftops, and steeples along the green hilly shore of Ireland. Ten minutes later, Turner picked up a 245-foot, loaf-life promontory, the Old Head of Kinsale. Its lighthouse was unmistakable.

The master knew now where he was but not precisely how far offshore. This could have had some relevance for his arrival off Liverpool Bar, since he did not want to lay-to waiting for high tide and a pilot. So he ordered a 4-point bearing upon Kinsale. This meant the liner would have to be held for some forty minutes at a fixed speed (18 knots presently) on an undeviating course, now 87 degrees east.

At 1:50 P.M. Third Officer Albert A. Bestic commenced the bearing. The liner was kept steady on course, which, as a matter of fact, would have taken her into Cork Harbor in two hours. In so doing, Turner was ignoring a number of instructions: "Give prominent headlands a wide berth . . . fast steamers can considerably reduce the chance of successful surprise submarine attacks by zigzagging . . . pass harbors at full speed . . . steer mid-channel course." The *Lusitania's* skipper knew about zigzagging, but he was under the impression it was to be applied only after a U-boat was sighted.

About the same time, Schwieger had surfaced to likewise take a bearing on the Old Head of Kinsale. He logged the unexpected sighting of "four funnels and two masts of a steamer . . . ship is made out to be a large passenger steamer." He ordered the U-2 down to periscope depth while keeping watch on his new potential target.

Aboard the big Cunarder passengers who weren't packing for the next day's scheduled docking in Liverpool were finishing lunch or enjoying the sun and scenery on deck. In the first class dining saloon, for example, where the string orchestra was whining through "The Blue Danube," Theodate Pope and a thirty-two-year-old fellow spiritualist Edwin Friend were expressing amusement at the plight of an Englishman seated across from them who had been served a dish of ice cream minus a spoon. Robert Timmins, a cotton dealer from Texas, not only managed to finish his ice cream, but ordered more. "We've got time," he laughed.

Theodate and Friend excused themselves and left. Others lingering over coffee included Dorothy Conner, also Lady Mackworth and her father, D. A. Thomas, former Liberal member of Parliament. C. T. Hill, at a nearby table, looked at his watch and decided, "I must hustle for I'm late." The tobacco man hurried to a lift to find Miss Gale, the ship's stenographer. He had letters to dictate.

At this time in London, Colonel Ed House, special adviser to President Wilson, was leaving Buckingham Palace after a brief appointment with King George V. "We fell to talking, strangely enough," the Texan and staunch Anglophile would note in his diary, "of the probability of Germany sinking a transatlantic liner. He [the King] said, "Suppose they should sink the *Lusitania* with American passengers on board.'" House had thought it "a curious remark" and intended to discuss it with Walter Hines Page, American ambassador to the Court of St. James.

On the U-20, Schwieger had been "hoping she [the liner] would change course to starboard along Irish coast." Incredulous, he watched the *Lusitania* do just that, then near him on a steady course, minute by minute. At 2:09 P.M. his armament officer reported, "Torpedo ready!" The towering Cunarder was no farther than half a mile distant. The commander gave the order: "Fire!"

Many on the *Lusitania* spotted the torpedo's approach. Probably the first was Leslie Morton, eighteen-year-old seaman on the forecastle watch. Turning toward the bridge he sang out, "Torpedoes coming on the starboard side!" Second Officer P. Hefford repeated the cry for the benefit of Captain Turner, who was on the port bridge wing, studying the Old Head. He started on the run for the opposite side. Jay Brooks, on the Marconi deck, as high as a passenger could reach, saw the wake at the same time. He grasped the rail and shouted, "Torpedo!" Florence Padley, in a deck chair, thought she was watching a porpoise swimming at unusual speed toward the ship. Alighting from the elevator on "B" deck, C. T. Hill was accosted by Jones, the chief steward in first class. "Good God, Mr. Hill, here comes a torpedo!" Hill raced on deck to the railing to see it vanish into the side of the liner. To Oliver Bernard, walking along the promenade deck, the unwelcome appearance was more subtle, something on the sea that "impinged on my mental focus."

Brooks watched the white streak of water disappear inside the hull far below him. At once, the large ventilator under No. 1 funnel and nearest the bridge geysered steam, water, coal, smoke, and other debris over his head. Though he sought shelter under the Marconi "shack," the eruption began falling, knocking him flat on his face. He thought he was going to suffocate.

On the U-20, Schwieger logged, "Shot hits starbound side right behind bridge. An unusually heavy detonation follows with a strong explosion cloud (high in the air over first smokestack). Added to the explosion of the torpedo there must have been a second explosion (boiler, coal, or powder)."

The sound of the explosion was distinct and different, from passenger to passenger: "like a million-ton hammer hitting a steel boiler"; "a jamming noise"; "that made by the slamming of a door . . . a dull, muffled explosion"; as though "from a mine, or that we had run on a rock"; "a heavy, rather muffled sound." In the second-class dining saloon, there was a noise only of shattering glass, as though "someone had fallen through a glass house," it seemed to Archibald Donald. Most stood up. There was some screaming and the thuds of those falling to the deck. Then the lights flickered out. The towering Reverend Gwyer arose with arms outstretched as if in a pulpit and suggested: "Let us quieten the people!" He urged the passengers to move calmly to the doors, assuring them, "Everything's going to be all right!"

On the bridge they knew better. Marconi operator Robert Leith was already tapping out: "Come at once. Big list . . . 10 miles south Old Head Kinsale." He was only guessing the *Lusitania's* position. None yet knew her location exactly. The stricken liner was plunging ahead from her own momentum, out of control, in a wide arc, veering to port. She would not answer the helm; the steam lines had likely been ruptured.

That the Cunarder was under way and listing to starboard —at times as much as 25 degrees—made it very difficult to lower lifeboats. Those on the port side could not be launched at all, swinging inboard onto the decks. In fact, at least one on the starboard side, improperly lowered (the bow line had slipped), spilled all of its occupants, mostly women and children, into the water. Among them was Mary, Odgen Hammond's wife. She had wryly observed, moments before, when she dropped her purse, "I guess I won't need this where we'll be going." In fact, Jay Brooks, who had survived the shower of debris, distinctly heard Captain Turner call out, "Lower no more boats! Everything is going to be all right!"

But the crew continued to try to launch them anyhow. Because of the list, one could almost walk from the starboard boat deck on the promenade deck right into the craft. Balancing against the slope of the deck, Brooks progressed aft to see perhaps as many as sixty women clutching the iron railing in frozen terror.

"Come on, ladies, I'll help you," he offered. Tall and strong, he assisted one after another into the waiting boat.

Curiously, perhaps, the tire chain salesman's relative calm was shared by others. In fact, throughout the doomed ship, settling lower and lower by the bow, panic was rare. A steward recognized Vanderbilt, for example, helping a young woman with her lifebelt. He shouted to the millionaire to "Hurry . . . or it will be too late!" Instead, Vanderbilt lit another cigarette and gazed out at the ever-nearing waters. In his hand he held what appeared to be a small ladies purse. Few were aware that the otherwise athletic young man couldn't swim a stroke.

Charles Lauriat, the Boston bookseller, who had been shuttling up and down to bring lifebelts (or "jackets") on deck from below, recognized Elbert and Alice Hubbard, holding hands, looking "very gray-haired," refusing to be assisted into a boat. It was the same "Fra Elbertus" who once had written, "We are here now. Some day we shall go . . . would like to go gracefully." They were observed strolling into a companionway, as if returning to their cabin.

Certainly none envinced the sangfroid of Charles Frohman as he lit a fresh cigar after removing his lifejacket and assisting a woman into it. Rita Jolivet, nearby, heard him remark, "Why fear death? It is the most beautiful adventure in life." She recognized the words from *Peter Pan.* James Barrie was the producer's friend and favorite author. It was distressingly obvious to the young actress that Frohman intended to do absolutely nothing to save himself.

Oliver Bernard, like Lauriat and other men, had moved against the surging tide of passengers in the corridors and stairways to procure lifebelts. Soon, he decided the ship couldn't last much longer, and that there would not be enough boats for everyone. He wanted to be in an advantageous location to jump and swim for it. So he climbed above the boat deck to the narrow Marconi deck from which Brooks had watched the torpedo.

Well away from the ship, he saw a man, almost naked, swimming slowly but with determination. This inspired Bernard to remove his coat, vest, collar and necktie. Then he folded them neatly and placed the bundle at the base of one of the funnels, aware as he did so of the absurdity of his action. As he untied his shoelaces, he was seized by an "awful sadness," a wearied sense of futility of life and its struggle for "petty attainments." What did it all mean?

Schwieger, on the other hand, observed: "Great confusion on board . . . many boats crowded come down bow first or stern first . . . the ship blows off, in front appears the name *Lusitania* in gold letters." And at 3:25 P.M. he added, "It seems as if the vessel will be afloat only a short time. Submerge to 24 meters and go to sea. I could not have fired a second torpedo into this throng of humanity."

On the *Lusitania,* Marconi operator Leith, who had been calling for help without pause, transmitted desperately: "Send help quickly. Am listing badly!" Help was on the way, but neither fast nor close enough. Admiral Hood had heard the message and his Coast Patrol was steaming out of Queenstown. From the same port, four small tugs were casting off moorings. One of them, as a matter of fact, was the ancient *Stormcock,* which had towed the *Great Eastern* to the breakers.

But it would take them two or three hours to reach the position of the torpedoed Cunarder. Larger vessels (a tanker, several passenger ships) in the Channel were also responding, but they too were about 40 miles distant. From the village of Kinsale itself, fishing boats, all under sail and without engines, were tacking out to sea, past the Old Head, where a number of onlookers had been watching the whole tragic spectacle. Singularly, perhaps, they had been on the commanding headland an hour or more before the *Lusitania* had appeared, distant as she was. Thus, some were aware that U-boats were operating in these waters.

Many passengers with little confidence in the boats or their availability were leaving the ship directly. Jay Brooks dove in, not bothering even to remove his shoes. Familiar with the log-choked Androscoggin in Maine, he thought the 50-degree Atlantic quite "mild." Timmins, the cotton broker, plunged so deeply that the waters became "black as the inside of a cow." From the pressure, he figured he must have gone "50 feet down."

Charles Lauriat, encountering groups of other men and women afloat, urged them to put their hands on one another's shoulders and try to keep together. Archie Donald found swimming under these imperiled circumstances "the most marvelous revelation." Buoyed by his life preserver, he had the illusion he was moving over the waters with great speed as he sought to distance himself from the ship. Fourteen-year-old Virginia Bruce Loney, tossed into the water by an overturned lifeboat, put her early swimming skills to good use. Nearby, twelve-year-old Avis Dolphin was thrown out of her lifeboat after two hysterical men jumped aboard. She successfully struck out for a raft.

Theodate Pope, wearing her straw hat, jumped from the ship with little effort. But, as she seemed not to surface, she thought, "This of course is the end of life for me." When she did come up, her head hit the keel of a lifeboat or debris and she lapsed into unconsciousness.

Margaret Mackworth, thinking she was 60 feet above the surface of the sea, likened the challenge to jumping off a roof. Then, in moments, the *Lusitania* sank deeper and green water was swirling about her feet. She almost floated off.

At 2:28 P.M., no more than eighteen minutes after she had been hit, *Lusitania*'s bridge was awash, forcing Captain Turner up into the signal halyards rigging. The bow of the Cunarder had hit bottom, only 300 feet below the surface, the great liner being close to 800 feet long. For moments she hung at a precipitous angle, her four massive propellers visible and still turning slowly besides the 65-ton rudder.

Those on the fantail, the after deck, were 100 feet in the air, too terrified of the height and the spectacle of a half-sunken liner and the hundreds of people in the water below them to jump. The *Lusitania* remained there, frozen in time, unreal.

Then, with ominous rumblings, she began to settle lower, first returning to even keel, next lying over on her starboard side. Masts, antennae, rigging, davits, ventilators and other protrusions struck those struggling to get away from this man-made monster thrashing in her death agonies.

Two, Margaret Gwyer and William H. Pierpont of Liverpool, actually were sucked into the funnels and blown forth again, shaken, blackened, but otherwise unhurt. Three others, Charles Lauriat, James Brooks, and Virginia Loney, managed to stroke away from the entangling antennae.

From a lifeboat, George Kessler turned to pronounce his own amen: "My God! The *Lusitania*'s gone!" Where she had been was only a mound of bubbling, foaming water and a field of debris defying description.

Those not lucky enough to be in a boat or the flimsier "collapsibles" seized whatever floated their way. Turner, a powerful swimmer, found salvation in a chair. Still wearing his pushed-down captain's cap, he dog-paddled towards shore at a reasonable pace.

Theodate Pope, after fighting off a large man who kept attempting to claw onto her shoulders, managed to straddle an oar. Lady Mackworth, first perching on a chicken coop, moved onto a large wicker chair. A small group of men grabbed a beer keg. Someone else had climbed onto a partially awash piano.

It was almost two hours before the first rescue vessels arrived: the naval auxiliary *Indian Prince* and trawler *Peel 12* out of Glasgow. These were followed during the next hour by the historic tug *Stormcock*, the trawler *Bluebell*, a harbor sidewheeler the *Flying Fish* and at long last, the flagship HMS *Juno*.

One survivor was not content merely with being rescued. Elizabeth Duckworth, of Taftville, Connecticut, who had proven a muscular rower, had just stepped onto *Peel 12* when she heard an officer in another lifeboat call for volunteers to man the oars in order to return to the scene. She was the first to respond.

By nightfall, the living and the dead from the torpedoed Cunarder were coming ashore, from Kinsale to Queenstown. The U.S. consul at the latter port, Wesley Frost wrote:

> We saw the ghastly procession of these rescue ships . . . under the flaring gas torches along the Queenstown waterfront . . . ship after ship would come up out of the darkness and sometimes two or three could be just described awaiting their turns in the cloudy night to discharge bruised and shuddering women, crippled and half-clothed men and a few wide-eyed little children . . . Women caught at our sleeves and begged desperately for word of their husbands, and men with choking efforts of matter-of-factness moved ceaselessly from group to group seeking a lost daughter or sister or even bride. Piles of corpses like cordwood began to appear among the paint kegs and coils of rope on the shadowy old wharves.

Death as always was especially impartial in taking the known and the little known: Elbert and Alice Hubbard, Alfred Gwynne Vanderbilt, Charles Frohman, Justus Forman, Marie Depage, Albert L. Hopkins, the entire Crompton family of eight including their governess, the Charles Plamondons, Mrs. Ogden Hammond, Father Basil Maturin, Mr. and Mrs. Allen Loney (leaving Virginia Bruce orphaned), Edwin Friend, the two beautiful twin daughters of Lady Marguerite Allen of Montreal, George Vernon and many more.

The figures dispassionately told the story: 1,198 dead (including 785 passengers) out of the 1,959 who had sailed aboard the *Lusitania.* The total represented but 300 less than had gone down with the *Titanic* three short years earlier. Of the 159 holding American passports, 124 were dead. Many children—94 out of 124—perished. Included were 35 infants, of whom all but four were lost.

Ambassador Page's fateful cable reached Washington in mid-afternoon the same Friday, allowing for the time difference. The stock market plummeted. Businesses on the east coast and in the midwest closed early. Stunned, the nation had not been dealt such a blow since the staggering defeat of the Union Army at Bull Run in 1861. The tragedy of the *Titanic* seemed somehow different. Might this lead to war, people on the street asked aloud.

At first gray and silent, President Wilson finally observed that there was such a thing as being "too proud to fight," that a nation could be "so right" it need not "convince others by force." Many disagreed, including segments of the U.S. press, which reacted vehemently. The New York *Sun*, for one, depicted the Kaiser fastening a medal around the neck of a mad dog as a small flag labeled "*Lusitania*" sank into the sea. (As a matter of fact, the Germans struck a medal to commemorate the sinking, dated, curiously, "5 May 1915.") The Philadelphia *North American* caricatured the helmeted Hohenzollern as a roaring monster drowning a woman with his bare hands.

German-American stores were pillaged. Blind, mindless rage was vented even against butchers displaying sausages, whose windows were smashed, and the owners of harmless little dachshunds.

The attempted German justification that the *Lusitania* was armed and carrying all sorts of contraband including munitions was not only preposterous, it further inflamed America. Editorialists derided the German Ambassador Count Johann von Bernstorff who called at the White House to profess "deep regrets." For all his Prussian, moustached formidability, he was a man of peace who had tried to keep his government from alienating the United States.

On May 13, the President replied with the first of the

"Wilson Notes," asking Germany to disavow such acts as the sinking of the Cunarder, and to give assurances against future attacks on unarmed merchant ships without warning. Former President Roosevelt was among those who complained that the message was too mild, while the pacifistic Secretary of State William Jennings Bryan thought it too strong and shortly resigned. Whether the note was too weak or too strong, Colonel House would be writing in his diary that "war with Germany is inevitable." Since U-boats were sinking an average of 133,000 tons of Allied shipping each month, more or less indiscriminately, House's prediction seemed not too farfetched.

On June 15, Lord Mersey, who presided over the *Titanic* inquiry, opened hearings in Westminster Hall, London, on the loss of the great Cunarder. As at the coroner's inquest in Kinsale, Captain Turner did not appear to comprehend the enormity of the tragedy, much less his own role in bringing it about. He admitted before an often incredulous board of naval and merchant marine officers that he had ignored, or at the least misunderstood, all of his instructions for danger zone navigation and that he did not know what giving headlands "a wide berth" really meant. He also claimed not to know the position indicated by the directions to steer a "mid-channel" course, the implications of "full speed," and, most damning, "with any certainty where you are," as Lord Mersey pressed him.

Incredibly, even at the inquest, the master was not only exonerated but praised as "a skilled and experienced man." The court placed the blame solely with the submarine commander even as U.S. public opinion placed it on the Kaiser's doorstep.

Neither the official finding, the burial of the dead nor the continuing exchange of diplomatic protests and attempted justifications could lay the torpedoing to rest. Its reverberations persisted.

On July 28, Inez Vernon, Rita Jolivet's sister and the widow of George Vernon, put on an evening dress that had been his favorite, her jewels, and makeup and seated herself before her dressing table in her New York apartment. She took a small revolver from the drawer, pointed it at her right temple, and pulled the trigger.

As "preparedness" strode boldly into the American vocabulary, there were those with the outspoken conviction that if anyone were to die it better be "the Hun." Among them were old war horses like General Leonard Wood and Teddy Roosevelt, former Rough Riders at San Juan Hill, who organized a "business men's" training camp at Plattsburg, New York. Together with such middle-aged celebrities as Bernard Baruch and Richard Harding Davis (who would die the next year at fifty-two), they puffed and sweated through the manual of arms or, worse, obstacle courses which provoked mainly bruises, sprains, and a few fractures.

The Kaiser's undersea navy seemed bent on giving these men inspiration to march, with the torpedoing of the United States steamer *Leelanaw* on July 27 off Scotland but no loss of life. Another U-boat sank the *Arabic* in the Irish Channel on August 19. Two of the forty-five who died were American. Ambassador von Bernstorff disavowed the act.

German myopia with respect to the feelings—and importance—of neutrals proved nothing short of incalculable. On October 12, a firing squad in occupied Brussels executed Edith Cavell, a forty-nine-year-old English nurse who was matron of a nursing school and clinic. She had been charged with hiding Allied soldiers and men of military age and helping them to escape. The founder of the establishment was Dr. Antoine Depage, whose wife Marie had been lost on the *Lusitania*.

The national spasm of outrage following the sinking was rekindled. The New York *Tribune*'s "atrocity cartoon" was certainly the most violent of any. It depicted the Kaiser as a screaming werewolf holding a huge smoking pistol over the

Pages from *Harper's Weekly* of August 12, 1865 illustrating the *Great Eastern*'s first attempt at laying the transatlantic telegraph cable. (A.T.&T. Corporate Archives)

The British ship, *Great Eastern,* successfully placed the first telegraph cable from England to Newfoundland in 1866. (A.T.&T. Corporate Archives)

In 1819 the 320-ton *Savannah* became the first steamship to cross the Atlantic. Pathetically underpowered, she used her paddles only three days out of a month-long voyage. If imperfectly understood and appreciated at the time, the little vessel was nonetheless a harbinger of a new era in sea transportation. (Naval Historical Center)

One of the most famous of a handsome breed, the clippers, the *Flying Cloud* set some sort of a record on almost every voyage. One of her masters, Captain Josiah Creesy, became as renowned as his ship. (Naval Historical Center)

Chow time on the USS *Monitor,* July 1862. Very few pictures of the famous little ship survive. This one affords an impression of the turret, if not its cannon or gunports. Note the awning, a must for summertime on the James River. (Library of Congress)

If a photograph of the CSS *Merrimack* were ever taken, it has never been found. This is an artist's sketch made in 1898. (Naval Historical Center)

John Ericsson, inventor of the *Monitor*, was a proud, difficult, and often arrogant genius. But the craft he initially described to President Lincoln as a "battery" was destined to change history. (Naval Historical Center)

The handsome steam frigate USS *Minnesota* surely would have been destroyed by the rampaging *Merrimack* had not the tiny *Monitor* come to her rescue. (Naval Historical Center)

She was the largest creation to furrow the North Atlantic since the *Great Eastern*: RMS *Lusitania*, 32,000 tons, 790 feet overall. Her four steam turbines drove four propellers, making possible speeds in excess of 30 knots. Note that her forward funnel is "cold," as it was on her ill-fated final voyage. (Naval Historical Center)

Postcards of the *Lusitania*, like this one, were carried aboard for the use of passengers. Florence Padley, who was five months pregnant at the time of the torpedoing, survived the sinking and saved this one. (Author's collection)

The Imperial German Embassy in Washington inserted this paid warning notice in several New York newspapers May 1, 1915, the day of the sailing of the *Lusitania*. It seemed more than coincidence that the *World*, for one, positioned it next to the Cunard sailing schedule, another advertisement.

NOTICE!

TRAVELLERS intending to embark on the Atlantic voyage are reminded that a state of war exists between Germany and her allies and Great Britian and her allies; that the zone of war includes the waters adjacent to the British Isles; that, in accordance with formal notice given by the Imperial German Government, vessels flying the flag of Great Britian, or of any of her allies, are liable to destruction in those waters and that travellers sailing in the war zone on ships of Great Britian or her allies do so at their own risk.

IMPERIAL GERMAN EMBASSY,
WASHINGTON, D. C., APRIL 22, 1915.

RUSSIAN AMERICAN LINE
Only direct line to RUSSIA
1ST CLASS, $90.
2D CABIN, $65.
Regular Fortnightly service to Archangel.
A. E. JOHNSON & CO., Agts., 27 Bway, N.Y.

ANCHOR LINE

CUNARD
EUROPE VIA LIVERPOOL
LUSITANIA
Fastest and Largest Steamer now in Atlantic Service Sails
SATURDAY, MAY 1, 10 A. M.
Transylvania - Fri., May 7, 5P.M
Orduna, - - Tues., May 18, 10A.M
Tuscania - - - Fri., May 21, 5 P.M
LUSITANIA, - Sat., May 29, 10A.M
Transylvania, - Fri., June 4, 5PM
Gibraltar—Genoa—Naples—Piraeu
S.S. Carpathia, Thur., May 13, Noo
ROUND THE WORLD TOURS
Through bookings to all principal Ports of the World.
Company's Office, 21-24 State St., N. Y.

STEAMBOATS.
THE PUBLIC BE PLEASED.
COLONIAL LINE
BOSTON via Boat and Rail $2.60
PROVIDENCE Boat Direct $1.60

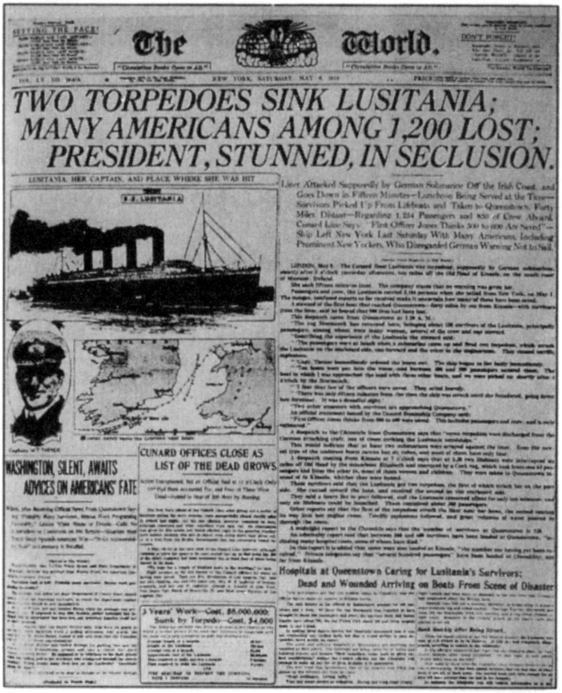

The World.

TWO TORPEDOES SINK LUSITANIA; MANY AMERICANS AMONG 1,200 LOST; PRESIDENT, STUNNED, IN SECLUSION.

LUSITANIA, HER CAPTAIN, AND PLACE WHERE SHE WAS HIT

WASHINGTON, SILENT, AWAITS ADVICES ON AMERICANS' FATE

CUNARD OFFICES CLOSE AS LIST OF THE DEAD GROWS

Hospitals at Queenstown Caring for Lusitania's Survivors; Dead and Wounded Arriving on Boats From Scene of Disaster

Americans awoke on Saturday, May 8, to the incredible news that the mighty *Lusitania* was lost. The early estimate of 1,200 dead was but two persons more than the actual figure, remarkably accurate reporting early in the twentieth century.
(The World)

Captain Turner of the *Lusitania* as he appeared on the streets of Queenstown, his uniform shrunken from immersion. Somehow, he kept his cap on the whole time he struggled in the frigid Atlantic, clinging to a chair. A powerful swimmer, he probably would have saved himself anyhow. (National Archives)

The survivors came ashore in Queenstown or Kinsale with what they wore, a few with what little they could carry. From the condition of their clothing, these six probably enjoyed the luxury of lifeboats. (National Archives)

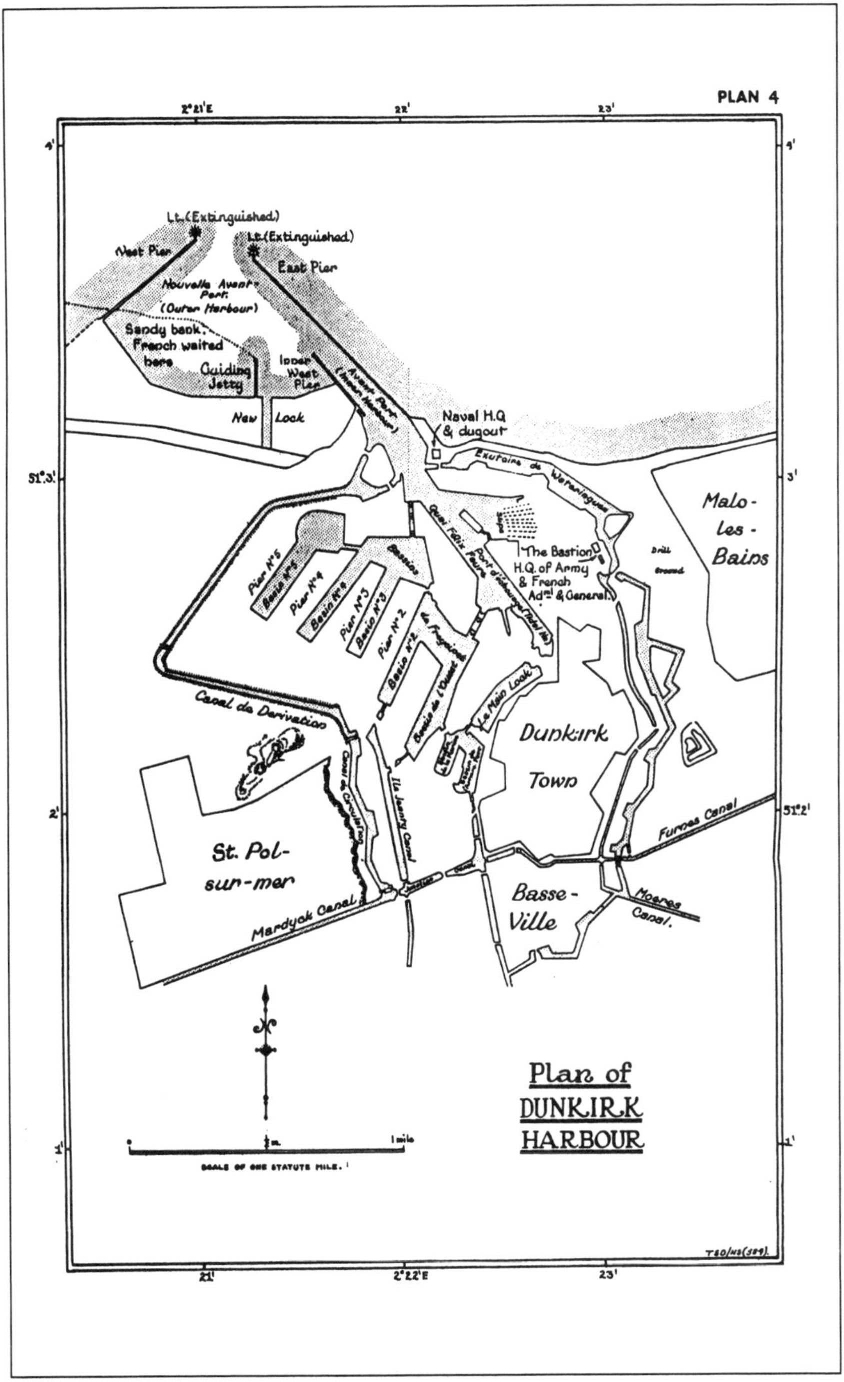

British map of Dunkirk harbor indicating the positions of the East and West piers which played so important a role in the evacuation. (Naval Historical Branch, Ministry of Defence, London)

"All the News That's Fit to Print."

The New York Times.

LATE CITY EDITION

NEW YORK, THURSDAY, MAY 30, 1940.

THREE CENTS

ALLIES ABANDONING FLANDERS, FLOOD YSER AREA; A RESCUE FLEET AT DUNKERQUE; FOE POUNDS PORT; ONE FORCE CUT OFF FROM THE SEA AS LILLE FALLS

PRESIDENT TO ASK $750,000,000 MORE FOR ARMY PROGRAM

Nazi Blitzkrieg Held to Show the $3,300,000,000 Allotted Fails to Meet Needs

FOR TANKS, GUNS, PLANES

Tax Bill to Be Offered in House Today—D. M. Nelson Named Procurement Director

ALLIES STRIKE FOR COAST IN EVER-TIGHTENING POCKET

NAZIS TIGHTEN TRAP

They Drive a Line Across Pocket, Encircling Foes in South

SAY YPRES IS TAKEN

Zeebrugge and Ostend Fall—Large Stores Are Reported Seized

The International Situation

COAST FIGHT RAGES

Communications Lines and Bases Bombarded Constantly by Nazis

DUNKERQUE SHELLED

Allies Inflicting Heavy Losses as They Battle in Rear-Guard Actions

HULL ORDER SPEEDS PLANES TO ALLIES

Allows Our Pilots to Fly Craft Over Three Canadian Maritime Provinces

Berlin Exchange Slumps As Optimism Is Decried

ITALY BARS IMPORTS EXCEPT BY BARTER

Cancels Permits to Bring In Goods or to Buy Exchange for Payments Abroad

URUGUAY ON GUARD FOR FIFTH COLUMN

Check on Assembly, Increase in Army Urged—Nazis Take Bold Tone in Ecuador

ALLIES GET NARVIK IN LAND-SEA FIGHT

Warships Support Troops in Final Thrust From Bels and Rombaks Fjords

HARRIED B. E. F. MEN ARRIVING IN BRITAIN

Many of Wounded Had to Wade Out to Boats Under Constant Fire of German Forces

11,000 Times Speedier Way Found To Obtain Atomic Power Element

Dispatches from Europe and the Far East are subject to censorship at the source.

Front page of New York *Times*.

These British and French soldiers did not make the evacuation. They are shown being taken prisoner by the Germans. (National Archives)

After Dunkirk and the fall of France, Hitler attempted to neutralize the RAF by bombing its bases. The strategy came very close to succeeding. When it did not, the Luftwaffe directed its full venom against British cities. This dramatic photograph shows St. Paul's Cathedral seemingly unscathed amidst a sea of flames. At one time, a 500-pound bomb penetrated the dome and buried itself in the chancel floor. Its subsequent removal won a George Cross for John Coote of Scotland Yard. (Library of Congress)

At 31,400 tons displacement and 608 feet in length, the USS *Arizona* was sleek, a beautiful battleship. Although commissioned in 1916, she was modernized in the 1930s with heavier antiaircraft guns and additional armor at the waterline. (Naval Historical Center)

". . . a whining sound, followed by a tremendous explosion that caused the ship to virtually rise out of the water, shudder and start settling down by the bow..." The forward powder magazine had been detonated by a bomb. The *Arizona* was destroyed. (National Archives)

A gleaming white marble memorial rests atop the wreck of the *Arizona*. Ghost-like, the outlines of the once proud battleship are plainly visible—the tomb of almost 80 percent of her crew. (Courtesy 14th Naval District)

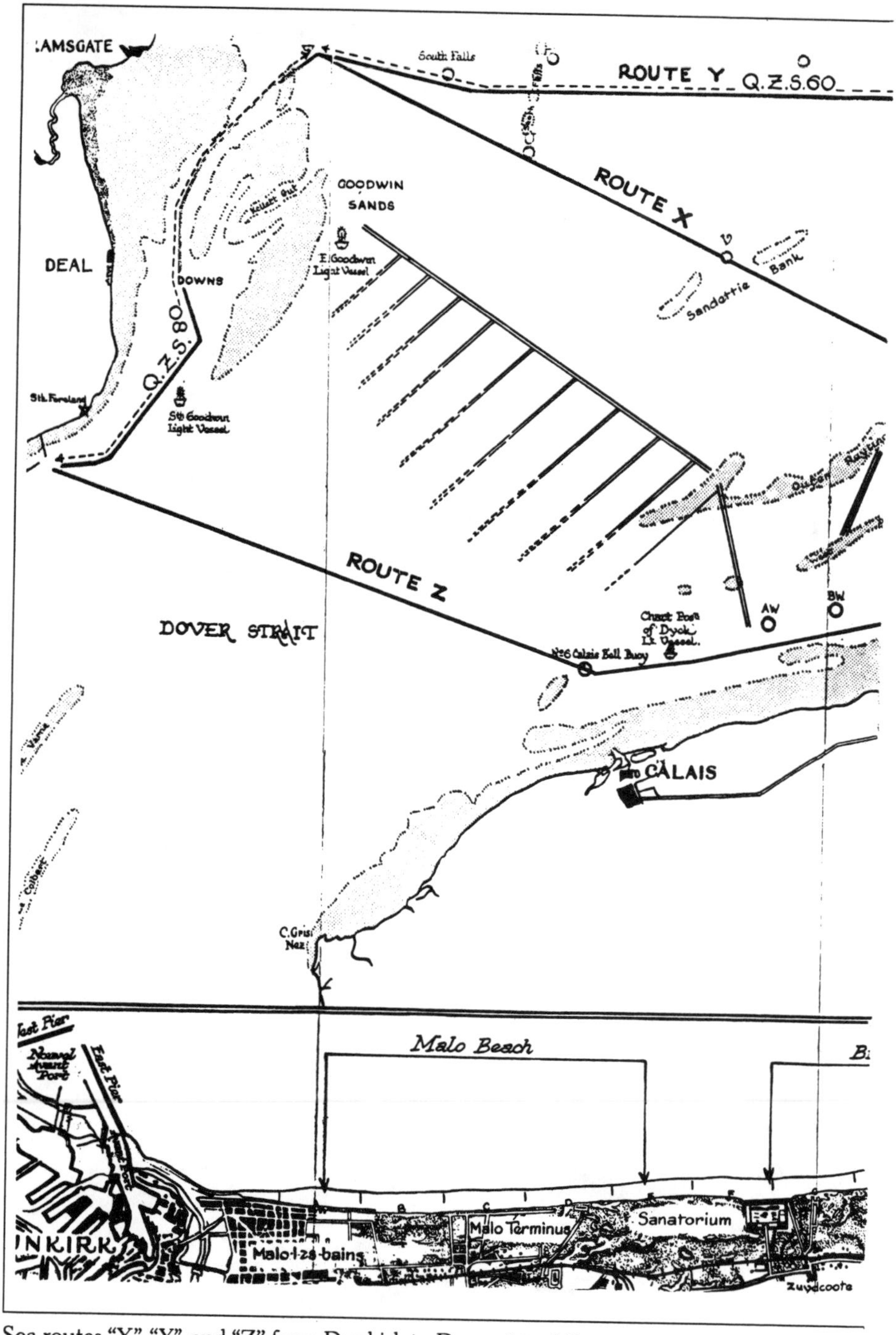

Sea routes "X", "Y", and "Z" from Dunkirk to Dover. (Naval Historical Branch, Ministry of Defence, London)

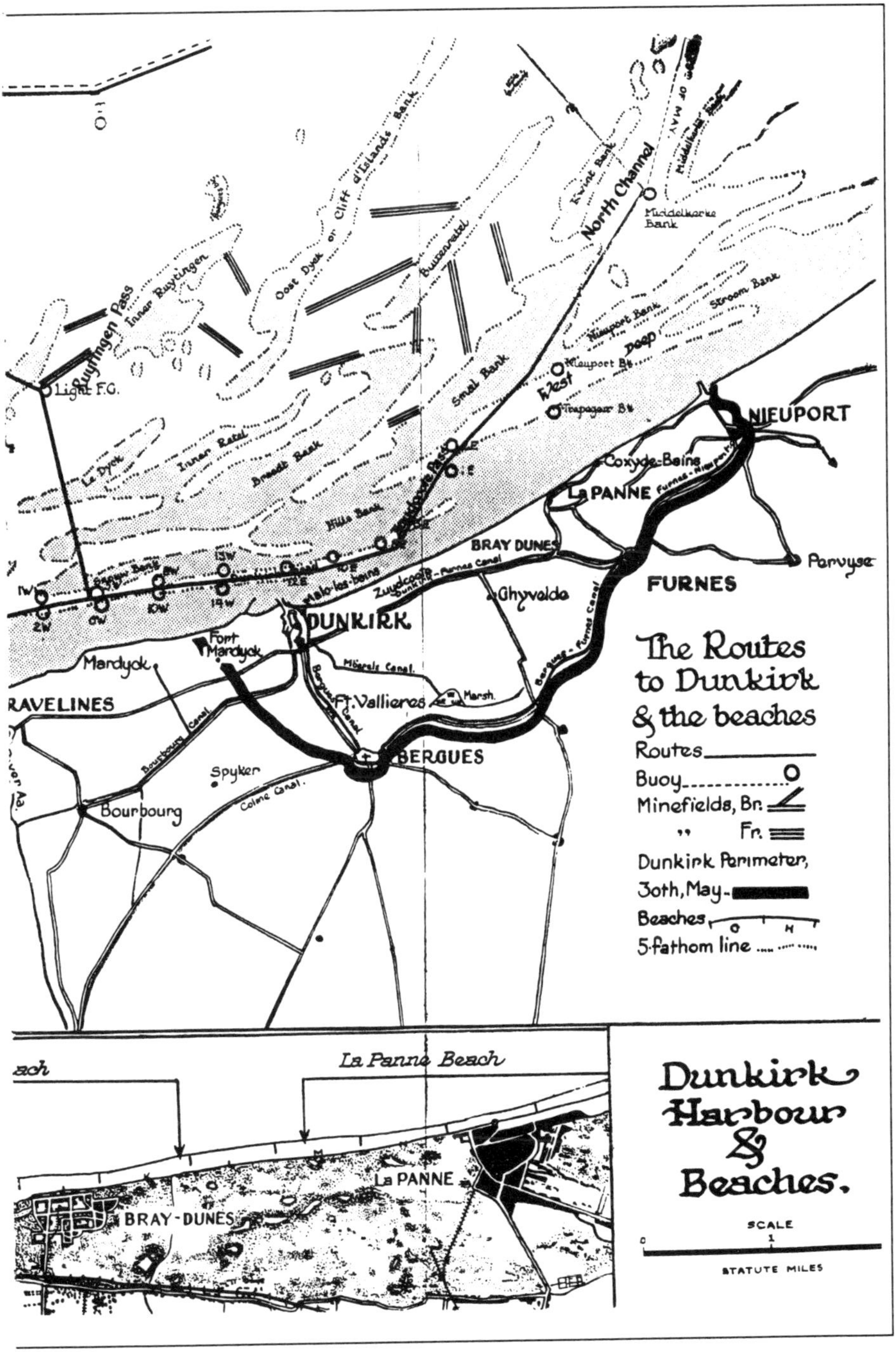

The Routes to Dunkirk & the beaches
Routes
Buoy
Minefields, Br.
" Fr.
Dunkirk Perimeter, 3oth, May
Beaches
5 fathom line
North Channel
Ruytingen Pass
Inner Ruytingen
Oost Dyck or Cliff d'Islands Bank
Buitenratel
Middelkerke Bank
Nieuport Bank
Stroom Bank
West Deep
Nieuport Bt.
Smal Bank
Inner Ratel
Le Dyck
Breedt Bank
Hills Bank
Light F.C.
NIEUPORT
Coxyde-Bains
LA PANNE
BRAY DUNES
FURNES
Parvyse
Zuydcoote
Ghyvelde
DUNKIRK
Fort Mardyck
Mardyck
RAVELINES
Ft. Vallieres
Marsh.
BERGUES
Spyker
Bourbourg
Bourbourg Canal
Colme Canal
Bergues - Furnes Canal
La Panne Beach
LA PANNE
BRAY-DUNES
Dunkirk Harbour & Beaches.
SCALE
0
1
STATUTE MILES

bleeding body of a woman. It was captioned "Gott mit Uns!" The White House was deluged with furious letters, of which this from a real estate operator in Lake Wales, Florida, was typical: "In the name of God and humanity, are we to stand back and witness . . . women nurses being shot by order of the German government for aiding dying and maimed soldiers to reach their homes?" Wilson himself decided, if reluctantly, that the nation needed an army "ready for war."

At a time when England was hurting for more volunteers, the "Boche" had provided yet another reason for fighting. Recruiters barked at rallies throughout the country, "Who'll avenge Nurse Cavell?" Ten thousand Britons enlisted in one day alone.

The fact that many Americans, like Allen Loney who had gone down with the *Lusitania*, were ambulance drivers in France was dramatized anew on Christmas eve when Richard Hall, another driver, was killed by a shell fragment. His death hardened the national resolve to do more to aid the Allied cause and, somehow, punish the "horrible Hun," a veritable beast on two legs who drowned little babies and murdered women. "Schrecklichkeit," a word which sounded as frightful as its very meaning, was the way the British described the Kaiser's brand of warfare: "Horror." The Americans seconded them whole-heartedly.

In response, Berlin published photographs of thin, starving children, with the caption claiming that the Allied blockades of the North Sea and Mediterranean were wholly responsible for their suffering. A continuing disdain for the rights and sensibilities of neutrals marked the Central Power's waging of war as 1916 commenced. The cry for "Preparedness" if not actual intervention was rising towards a climax. On March 24, the *Sussex*, a French cross-Channel steamer, was torpedoed without warning, causing the loss of American lives. It might have provided the final impetus to the organization the next month, of the Lafayette Escadrille, a group of young Americans, mostly college students, who would fly with the French air force.

On the first anniversary of the *Lusitania's* torpedoing, the New York *Herald* published a special edition with black-bordered columns as it had a year before. Editorially, it deplored the fact that Germany had not "atoned" for its act. A week later, on May 13, the women of Manhattan organized a mammoth rally and marched through the night. Sister preparedness paraders shouted and sang in other cities, winding along streets lit by the torches they brandished. Though he somehow seemed out of character with his straw hat, pince-nez, and inescapably academic face, President Wilson himself, holding an American flag, led a similar parade in Washington the following month.

Not only had Americans been driving for the Red Cross since early in the war, but some of them had actually been fighting in the trenches alongside the British and French, neutrality laws aside. For them it had not only proven a holy crusade; they had also acquired a morbid fascination with death itself, as though seduced. Exhilarated by war, they looked upon it as a very substance of life, indeed a goal for existence. "But I've a rendezvous with Death . . . and I to my pledged word am true, I shall not fail that rendezvous," wrote Alan Seeger, Harvard Class of 1910. He did not, struck down on July 4, 1916, near Belloy-en-Santerre.

The same month, Captain Charles Fryatt, master of the British merchant ship *Brussels,* was executed in Bruges, Belgium, for attempting to ram a U-boat. The Germans had charged this middle-aged father of seven with being a *franc tireur,* a civilian attacking the military. When Great Britain threatened to shoot German prisoners of war in retaliation, the enemy replied it would shoot two Allied prisoners for each German executed. A blood bath was averted when no more merchant captains were condemned by military courts.

Also in July the huge Black Tom munitions pier and complex in New Jersey was destroyed by German saboteurs. The tremendous blast was heard in Manhattan and by everyone living within a 50-mile radius. Although it was not confirmed until many months later, Americans were certain of the origins of this act. The explosion had been the work of a group led by Captain Franz von Papen, military attaché of the German embassy, which had manufactured at least 400 fire bombs aboard the interned liner *Friedrich der Grosse* to be placed on outgoing merchant vessels. (Von Papen would briefly be German chancellor in 1932.)

This major act of sabotage further fueled America's growing frustration with its role as a neutral. Roosevelt berated "broomstick preparedness." Ambassador Page bluntly denounced the maintenance of a position of neutrality "while the world is bleeding to death." Yet there were no further provocations until January 11, 1917, when a giant plant in Kingsland, New Jersey, manufacturing fuses for Russia, blew sky high with a force comparable to that of Black Tom. After that, history accelerated.

Germany appeared, in January, to be winning the war of the sealanes: More than 500,000 tons of merchant shipping was sent to the bottom every thirty days. Thus, Chancellor Theodore von Bethmann-Hollweg, a reasonable man who sought a negotiated peace, was overruled by the naval command, which held that unrestricted submarine warfare would win the war, a policy known as *spurlos versenkt!*—sunk without a trace.

On January 31, von Bernstorff delivered to Secretary of State Robert Lansing a terse announcement that "all sea traffic will be stopped with every available means and without further notice." One United States ship, following a prescribed course and carrying no contraband, would be allowed into Falmouth each Sunday.

That did it. On February 3, President Wilson advised a joint session of Congress that "diplomatic relations between the United States and the German Empire are severed." Von Bernstorff was handed his passport.

Even as Wilson spoke that Saturday afternoon, the 3,000-ton American freighter *Housantonic* was destroyed off the Scilly Islands by shellfire. The crew had first been permitted to abandon. Barely a week later, the schooner *Lyman M. Law* out of Bangor was torpedoed in the Mediterranean; her crew of tough old sailing salts made it to shore. Then, on Sunday evening, February 25, the Cunarder *Laconia*, at 18,000 tons now the largest liner in transatlantic service, was sunk while steaming at full speed in a blinding snowstorm towards Liverpool. She carried a crew of 216 and 73 passengers.

Those who had gathered in the first-class lounge were serenaded by "Poor butterfly" whining its tinny notes from "the talking machine," wrote one of the travelers, Floyd Gibbons. The famed correspondent had been listening to a passenger estimate that the chances of being struck by a torpedo were "four thousand to one" when "the ship gave a sudden lurch sideways and forward. There was a muffled noise like the slamming of some large door at a good distance away . . . I looked at my watch . . . 10:30 P.M. . . . then came the five blasts on the whistle."

The torpedo had hit on the starboard. It was followed about thirty minutes later by a second, after all had taken to the boats. "The ship sank rapidly at the stern," wrote Gibbons, "until at last its nose stood straight in the air. Then it slid silently down and out of sight like a piece of disappearing scenery in a panorama spectacle."

Among those lost were Mrs. Mary E. Hoy, of Chicago and her daughter Elizabeth. They froze to death in a lifeboat in waters not far from where the *Lusitania* had sunk. Mrs. Hoy's son, Austin, an American businessman in London, cabled President Wilson: "My beloved mother and sister have been foully murdered on the high seas . . . I call upon my government to preserve its citizens' self-respect and save others of my countrymen from such deep grief as I now feel."

Even before the President received the much-publicized appeal, he was signing into law an "armed neutrality" measure. Its first results would be the mounting of guns on U.S. flag ships.

"Declare war!" editorialized the New York *Tribune.* "Germany is already waging war against us" thundered Colonel "Marse" Henry Watterson, a Confederate veteran and the editor of the Louisville *Courier-Journal.* Billy Sunday, the evangelist, added his strident voice to those of many more conservative preachers who demanded immediate intervention. St. Luke's Episcopal Church, Manhattan, was one of a number to conduct special "military services," featuring choirs marching aggressively behind American flags up and down the aisles. Preachers in towns and cities throughout the land thumped for a "holy crusade" until Woodrow Wilson observed in disbelief to a friend, "Our ministers are going crazy!" They surely were seconded by the laity, who stepped up the tempo of preparedness parades, day and night.

The Kaiser's Germany apparently could not have cared less. In early March a cable was intercepted from Arthur Zimmerman, Berlin's foreign minister, to his legation in Mexico, suggesting that if peace with the United States failed, "We propose an alliance . . . with Mexico: that we shall make war together . . . we shall give general financial support and it is understood that Mexico is to reconquer the lost territory of New Mexico, Texas and Arizona."

This preposterous bit of "diplomacy" was exacerbated in mid-March by the sinking of one American flag vessel after another: the liner *Algonquin,* the freighters *Vigilancia* and *City of Memphis,* and the tankers *Illinois* and *Healdton.* All told, thirty-six United States citizens perished.

Shortly thereafter on Palm Sunday, April 1, the *Aztec* (of American registry) was nearing Le Havre with a full cargo of food. As the old freighter struggled through heavy seas and blinding rain squalls there was "a brilliant flash forward" and a shudder; the overladen vessel took such a list that it was almost impossible to launch boats, much less man the newly-mounted naval rifles. Twenty-seven crew members, more than half of her complement, and one Navy gunner died.

The next evening, as he spoke before Congress, the President had not yet heard of this latest in a dreary succession of sinkings and outrages. All of these acts would be traced back to the *Lusitania*, argued author Owen Wister, and they had been quickly compounded by the execution of Edith Cavell: "If there had been a possibility that American sympathy might be so divided as to hold us back from our duty and our salvation, that possibility was killed forever."

It was nearly 10:00 P.M. when Wilson returned to the White House through a city vibrant with a sense of destiny. The people lined Pennsylvania Avenue to cheer and wave hats and handkerchiefs as his heavy limousine rolled by. The grimfaced scholar was profoundly affected by the ovation. "My message today," he confided to his secretary, Joseph Tumulty in the cabinet room, "was a message of death for our young men. How strange it seems to applaud that." Then, according to the diminutive Tumulty, Woodrow Wilson put his head on the table and wept.

Recruiting tents sprouted up from coast to coast and little flags fluttered from street lamps, house windows, automobiles, and horse carts as the Senate debated the war resolution. It was passed 82-6. At 2:45 A.M. Good Friday, April 6, the House of Representatives started the roll call. The vote was 373–50 in favor. America was in the war.

"On the Western Front that day," wrote the historian Walter Millis, "in Italy and the Balkans, along the crumbling battle lines in Russia, in the far north and in the tropics and on the gray seas, the war had mangled its usual number of human bodies, inflicted its usual hurts and tortures, closed another day in its long, routine tale of agony. But all that, for the moment, was very far away. America, men simply thought, was in the war; and among them all, none quite knew how it had happened, nor why, nor what precisely it might mean."

Millis may also not have known in 1935 when his powerful, cynical *Road to War* was published. Not until the conflict's continuance (which would be called World War II), when the forces of consummate evil had become fully manifest and the United States had left Main Street forever, did the earlier great struggle seem perhaps just a bit more comprehensible.

And never had one ship set in motion such a mounting chain of actions and reactions that would forever change the course of history and put an end to a young nation's innocence.

Postscript: Neither Schwieger nor the U-20 survived the war. Then the sixth-ranking German submarine ace, the Kapitanleutnant who sank the *Lusitania* was lost in September 1917 while commanding the U-88 in a minefield off Denmark. The U-20 was depth-charged and destroyed in much the same waters. In 1984, divers dispatched by the author Clive Cussler located the wreck of the U-20 off Jutland.

Chapter Five

The Ships of Dunkirk

"At daybreak on September 1, 1939 . . . the German armies poured across the Polish frontier and converged on Warsaw from the north, south and west," wrote the correspondent William L. Shirer. "It was a gray, somewhat sultry morning in Berlin, with clouds hanging low over the city." Peace had lasted not quite twenty-one years. This was the beginning of World War II, and of an initial Allied debacle of immeasurable proportions which culminated in the closing days of May 1940 on the flaming beaches of France and Belgium.

Inaction, however, during the winter of 1939–40, as opposing warriors stared at one another across the Maginot and Siegfried lines, led to the dangerous cynicism that this was a "phony war," a "Sitzkrieg." The almost total lack of belligerency was welcome manna to extreme pacifists in the United States such as Charles Lindbergh and Father Coughlin of the America First Committee and William Dudley Pelley of the Silver Shirts. Why should this nation have anything to do with a so-called war in a far-off land in which the participants themselves did not even want to fight?

On April 9, the illusion was shattered as the Nazis swept across Denmark and into Norway with little or no resistance. A month later, "Plan Yellow," the assault on the West, was activated. "Like a sharp scythe," in the phraseology of Winston Churchill, Marshal Gerd von Rundstedt bypassed the Maginot line to the north through the Ardennes forest, considered "impenetrable," while other Panzer tank units breached the French defenses farther south at Sedan, location of a similar disaster in the Franco-Prussian War, in 1870. Three days later, on May 13, the Netherlands was cut in two and Queen Wilhelmina fled to London. Rotterdam, an "open city," was bombed into rubble.

In the next week, the Dutch army surrendered, Brussels and Antwerp were occupied, and the Wehrmacht had driven 30 miles into France, racing towards Paris. Abbeville, a channel port on the Somme, fell. On May 28, King Leopold, without advising his allies, surrendered Belgium and his forces. Only belatedly had he requested help of the British Expeditionary Force (BEF) numbering about one-third million. This left the British and remnants of the French and Belgian armies in a rapidly narrowing pocket from Dunkirk on the French coast roughly 45 miles south to Lille. General Heinz Guderian, commanding Hitler's XIX Corps, spoke the truth when he described the stunning defeat as a "splendid success." To Churchill, as a new prime minister busily forming his war cabinet, it was a "hideous dilemma."

However, for several days prior to the Belgian collapse, London had been anticipating disaster and, in the few ways available, preparing to meet it. Predictions were the gloomiest. Churchill thought that at most only 30,000 men might be rescued. The commander of the BEF, General the Viscount Lord John Gort believed "a great part of the [force] and its equipment will inevitably be lost." Gort, a large, imposing figure at fifty-three, was the holder of the Victoria Cross awarded for bravery in 1918. But he could not work miracles. His only hope was to get his men to the beaches and back home. But how?

From a practical standpoint, the answer, if answer there were, rested upon the shoulders of the luckless naval officer who happened to command the nearest, major English port: Dover. And the gentleman was fifty-seven-year-old Vice

Admiral Sir Bertram Ramsay, who served in the vital Channel squadrons in the first World War. He was a small, quiet man who could function without sleep for an incredible length of time. His facade of imperturbability collapsed, however, when faced with incompetence. He could not suffer fools, and those who proved they were likened his sudden eruption of fury to the blast of a German 88mm cannon.

The historic, lofty old Dover Castle was his headquarters, home, and office. Long anticipating the fall of France and cross-Channel shelling by the Germans, the foresighted Ramsay had established his operations room in a sort of cave hacked out of the chalk cliffs beneath the castle. It was part of a labyrinth of casemates, dating to the Napoleonic wars. This was the admiral's "Dynamo Room," a sobriquet dating to the last war when the hideaway housed emergency generating equipment.

At about the time the Germans were storming into Abbeville, on May 20, Ramsay asked the Admiralty what sort of a rescue fleet he could expect if the BEF had to be evacuated. The answer was somewhat less than satisfactory: perhaps two dozen Channel ferries, six coastal cargo ships, and maybe a dozen fishing boats. Scarcely adequate for an army of half a million desperate men, and only enough, Ramsay estimated, to save about 45,000 of them.

There was good reason for this parsimony of adequate transports. The big liners, such as the *Queen Mary,* the new *Mauretania,* and the *Aquitania* of World War I vintage, each of which could embark an entire division, were far too tempting as targets and, as well, would have to lay to well offshore. Battleships and cruisers, too cumbersome for inshore operations, were needed in North Atlantic convoying, in the Mediterranean, and in the ill-starred Norway campaign.

This left the destroyers, minesweepers, minelayers, and the sort of "little ships" already offered the admiral. The most numerous and capacious of this latter category were the paddle steamers, which plied the Channel, harbors and rivers. Typical of the class was the *Medway Queen*, a sixteen-year-old grande dame of the Thames excursion run; she was 179 feet long, of 316 tons. Already converted into a minesweeper, she had swept the Thames Estuary.

"This was the bitter winter of 1939," recalled John Douglas Graves, a reservist and second in command, who was a consulting surveyor in civilian life. "Even the Estuary partly froze over, and for weeks on end a tug was required to go before us morning and night so that our paddles would not be damaged by the ice floes, which were sometimes quite large. The seas that came aboard froze, and decks and rails became coated with ice which had at times to be chipped away to restore stability. Day after day, the little ship plunged out into the North Sea, streaming her sweeps and searching the depths, returning home each night with little to report except that the shipping channels were clear."

Then, around mid-May the *Medway Queen's* routine was interrupted and she was ordered to stand by for new duties involving her former role of transporting people. Other "little craft" were being alerted. Even the staid BBC was suggesting in repeated broadcasts that owners of small boats contact the Admiralty. "Continual telephone conversations," Admiral Ramsay was to report, "took place between Dover, the Admiralty, Ministry of Shipping and the Commander-in-Chief Nore [another naval command on the Thames], as to the provision of small craft for the final evacuation and provisions of Naval personnel for manning the small boats required for ferrying and skoots [Dutch coastal craft] and other small vessels taken up for transport purposes."

Shipyards and yacht basins along the Thames erupted into life like fresh blossoms in springtime. One was the century-old yard of Douglas Tough at Teddington on the upper Thames. There and at nearby anchorages were some 150 yachts, cabin cruisers, and motor sailers, which met the

Admiralty's basic qualification of being more than 30 feet overall. Here were moored objects of a weekend sailor's affection such as *Our Lizzie, Kitcat, Blue Bird, Miss Modesty, Mata Hari* and *Sundowner.* A 52-footer, the last named belonged to Charles Lightoller, who had been second officer of the *Titanic.*

Engines were the biggest challenge, since many vessels had been laid up for the winter and most were designed for fresh water. At Tough's, this and other problems were the province of Robert Lenthall, senior warden of the yard. "We removed masts, loaded them with petrol tins and generally made room in 'em," he recalled. "Really wasn't much we could do, you know." He went to work on an initial flotilla of fourteen boats.

In most cases, owners such as Lightoller volunteered to pilot their craft wherever they were needed. Otherwise, naval reservists, being called up from their offices, stores, and elsewhere would take command. One of these hundreds was Ted Harvey, a fisherman from Leigh-on-Sea, Essex, assigned as coxswain aboard a 30-foot harbor launch, *Moss Rose,* at Sheerness, on the lower Thames. "All we had to do," he noted, "was to load up with red cheese, chocolate, and two-gallon petrol tins—and wait."

By now, however, May 24th, Ramsay had been assured of almost 130 of this uniquely assorted fleet. On the same day, Friday, German tanks were ordered to halt by Hitler himself on the Aa canal line, in some places in telescopic sight of the French and Belgian beaches. There appeared to be a number of reasons: battle losses, the need for reserves to come up, and necessary repairs. Crews were weary from their long, spectacular dash and the tanks had to be primed for the ultimate target, Paris. In addition, Air Marshal Hermann Goering had convinced his Fuehrer that the wonderful Luftwaffe by itself could finish off the remnants of the Allied armies.

The abrupt command, as might have been expected, was stunning, if not insulting to the German army, the Wehrmacht. General Heinz Guderian, commanding the XIX Panzer Corps, described himself as "utterly speechless." Most of the ground staffers had already come to hate the vain, arrogant Goering.

At the same time, word was sweeping through the British regiments, "Every man for himself! Make for Dunkirk!" "As we moved through La Panne," wrote Sergeant W. B. Giblett, with the Second Battalion, Wiltshire Regiment, "the sight of devastation was everywhere. Bombed buildings had toppled into the streets and masses of debris were scattered around while flames flared and crackled as houses and vehicles burned after a recent bombing attack.

"The road running along to Dunkirk was choked with wrecked and burned out vehicles, among them a number of Red Cross ambulances. Many of the vehicles had belonged to the French troops, though some had been in the area from the beginning, including a few British vehicles."

Once on the beach, Giblett looked around "at an incredible sight: thousands of men stretched in a long line ten or twelve men deep . . . along the water's edge were groups of men every few hundred yards, many of them had waded into the sea so that the foremost men had water almost at chest level as they waited patiently and hopefully . . . quite a number of vehicles had been run onto the beach and were scattered around, many of them burned out wrecks destroyed by bombing or shell fire."

Many of the residents had left so abruptly that food was still on the table. Lieutenant Commander Thomas "Tommie" Kerr, with a Royal Navy beach liaison party, would recall of one house near Bray, Belgium, "Inside it was neat, a meal laid for, just an abandoned home, with the kitten being fed sardines by my men."

On Sunday, May 26, just two days before Leopold capitulated, Admiral Ramsay recorded, "The military situation was thought to have deteriorated so rapidly that the Vice Admiral was informed by the Admiralty that it was imperative for 'Dynamo' to be implemented with the greatest vigour."

At 5:40 P.M., the War Office officially stamped the evacuation plan "Dynamo," and set it in motion about an hour later, noting, "A fleet of all sorts of craft is now under control of Vice Admiral Dover. Shipping could take over 30,000 a day which could not be lifted from beaches alone but might be stretched even further if bulk of movements were from ports say Dunkirk and Ostend."

The beachhead was now a bit over 21 miles long, commencing about 6 miles west of Dunkirk, including also Bray-Dunes in France, and La Panne, to the east, and Nieuport in Belgium. Its depth would soon be compressed to no more than 6 miles, and to only 2 miles in the Nieuport Bains sector.

"What a terrible night that was!" exclaimed Lieutenant Commander Tommie Kerr, "For we had gotten hold of the odds and ends of an army, not the fighting soldiers. There weren't any officers, and those there were useless . . . we worked without ceasing all the dark hours, restoring confidence . . . by speech and promise of safety and sight of our naval uniforms. Pathetic the faith in the Navy." Especially so, he might have added, since there were no ships at the moment awaiting them.

Kerr was ordered to Bray Beach to embark 5,000 men: "It took some time to get there by bomb-cratered road and wrong turnings . . . then we gave a gasp, 5,000? Not a bit of it, there must have been 25,000 at the very least!" Five transports had steamed from Dover that night, but were forced to turn back because of heavy shelling along the enemy-held coast from near Calais to Gravelines, at the western extremity of the beachhead. The rest of Ramsay's "Gilbert and Sullivan" navy, however, was being readied the night long. It seemed to Thomas R. Russell, chief cook aboard the *Medway Queen*, that enough "grub" was being stowed "to feed a ruddy army."

Monday, May 27, dawned calm and clear. The fleet as it

then existed, from ship's lifeboats to some of the Channel steamers, started out. The seaway was so jammed, according to Robert Lenthall of Tough's yard, that it was "just like Piccadilly." Among the assemblage was Ted Harvey's harbor launch, *Moss Rose,* without a compass, just playing "follow the leader."

All the way across, the sailors could see clouds of dirty black smoke rolling towards the North Sea. It turned out that the source was burning oil refineries, fired by the French to deny them to the enemy. They passed one of the few vessels that had been off the beaches—a "guardship"—and already was Dover-bound, the Isle of Man ferry, *Mona's Isle.* She had been machine-gunned by German fighter planes and shelled from shore, but stayed afloat while sustaining casualties. Of the more than 1,400 crowded aboard, 23 had been killed and 60 wounded.

The artillery shelling was severe on the beaches as well, especially near La Panne. The troops commenced to move towards Dunkirk, thinking it safer. The lucky ones carried the wounded on stretchers, some wading into the water in the hopes of finding a boat. Tommie Kerr was dumbfounded at "the sight of one little dinghy with 2,000 men waiting to get into it . . . we couldn't persuade the troops it was no quicker to stand in the water than on the dry sand. They always felt that someone would get in front."

Kerr rounded up a group of soldiers, then started them marching towards Dunkirk. Boarding a "drifter" (a small fishing boat) for a drink of tea, he had to duck for cover as "shells started coming in . . . then another terrific air raid of which only one lot of bombs were in any way frightening."

But the soldiers were already becoming used to the pummelling. He found one group sound asleep and a soldier "snoring his head off." Kerr had to shake them awake before resuming his patrol by car, soon to be machine-gunned by low-flying Messerschmitts: "The car was hit by only one bullet.

They go fast, it is quickly over, not so terrifying as you might think when you are doing something."

Ramsay's fleet had arrived by the shortest route, "Z," 39 miles long. The two longer routes, "X" (55 miles), and "Y" (87 miles), had the advantage of being well away from the German-held coasts. "Y" swung around the Kwinte Whistle Buoy, about 15 miles north of Ostend and kept well out into the North Sea all the way to Dover. The lighted buoy impartially aided friend and foe.

Ted Harvey made four trips in *Moss Rose*, ferrying troops from the beach to larger ships. Otherwise, a major point of embarkation in deeper water was the cement and stone East Pier, or Jetée de l'Est, 1,400 yards long, although it was only five feet wide and planked with wood, known as a quay or mole, serving as a breakwater. Near the long East Pier, the *Moss Rose* was rammed on her last shuttle, though she made it to shallow water before settling to the bottom.

Without a boat, Harvey passed the time for a bit playing football with a group of soldiers. Afterwards, he noticed a few of them going over to a mound of corpses, first poking at them with sticks, turning them over. Soon they were looting the pockets of the dead, seeking mostly paper francs. Harvey thought, "I don't want to get like them."

By now, Ramsay's senior aide, Captain William G. Tennant, had been landed by the destroyer *Wolfhound*, after being attacked by air most of the way. As senior naval officer at Dunkirk, he was charged with organizing the men on the beaches for evacuation. He enjoyed but two means of communication to his admiral, ship's wireless and a miraculously intact telephone cable to Dover connected to the ancient switchboard of the Ambassador Hotel, La Panne. Tennant at once reported: "Port consistently bombed all day, and on fire . . . please send every available craft to beaches east of Dunkirk immediately."

So far, less than 10,000 troops had reached England. The greatest loss this Monday night was the big Dover-Calais ferry

Queen of the Channel, sunk in a single dive-bomber attack. However, most of the some 950 aboard were rescued.

The surrender of King Leopold during the first minutes of Tuesday, May 28, should have come as no surprise, least of all to President Roosevelt, since his ambassador to Belgium, John Cudahy, had already advised him that the ruler was "going to pieces like a wornout rope." Lord Gort, in an understatement, telephoned "Dynamo" that the situation was perilous.

Ramsay's operational board indicated that "2 transports, 9 destroyers, 4 minesweepers, *Calcutta* (an antiaircraft cruiser) 17 drifters and a few skoots" should at this early hour be off the beaches. Obviously, they weren't enough. He contacted all adjacent naval commands to round up every "shallow draught" boat that could be found, confiscating them if necessary, and postscripted, "Commander-in-Chief Nore at this stage provided additional reinforcements of minesweepers and paddlers."

Eight "paddlers," part of the Tenth Minesweeping Flotilla, set out from Dover, the flag of the Sub-Divisional leader aboard the *Medway Queen.* They also included the *Brighton Belle, Gracie Fields, Laguna Belle, Princess Elizabeth, Queen of Thanet, Sandown, Thames Queen.* "In line ahead they steamed through the night to a point about half a mile from the shore where, in the first faint light of dawn could be made out long lines of men standing still like human piers stretching out into the water—knee, waist even neck high in it; standing so patiently there in full equipment, boots, rifles, packs, tin helmets and all . . . orders were to leave by daylight but in the face of what we found this was not possible, and as dawn broke, the ships put off their life boats to be rowed or towed to the heads of the human queues."

The *Calcutta* stood by, giving antiaircraft protection, but the major attack did not develop until after 7:00 A.M., when the paddlers started back for Dover. The *Medway Queen* herself shot down one of the estimated 100 dive bombers hurtling at the flotilla. In the confusion, the *Brighton Belle* drifted over a submerged wreck and slowly sank; the *Medway Queen* rescued all aboard.

Ashore, Sergeant Giblett reported, "The number of men on the beaches declined only slowly and the queue remained just as long and seemingly as big as ever. Every once or twice an hour there would be a bombing raid with the planes dropping bombs onto and machine gunning the beaches or as an alternative there would be shelling and mortaring of some part of the beach. These attacks meant instant dispersal to any possible cover where we remained for awhile before the queue reformed with everyone taking up his original place; there was no attempt at queue jumping. . . . we watched the struggle between our ships at sea and the enemy planes attacking them. We could see quite clearly the bombs dropping toward their targets and the flash of tracer from machine guns; great plumes of water rose alongside the ships as bombs exploded in the water nearby."

The Royal Air Force (RAF) was boldly tearing into the Luftwaffe formations, hopelessly outnumbered, taking toll of the enemy while sustaining their own casualties. The sergeant observed "the flash of flames as a plane caught fire, the scream of engines as it dived out of control, a pilot dropping to earth on a parachute, tracer lines in the sky." What none on the shore could appreciate was the fact that much of the aerial action took place inland as the RAF sought to obliterate the Luftwaffe on the ground, hurriedly occupying captured Belgian and French airdromes.

At La Panne, naval officer Tommie Kerr spotted "a blazing ship full of soldiers" far offshore. He was frustrated that he could do nothing about it. Then he was compelled to give an order he thought he'd never have to issue: the summary execution of a spy, a man posing as a fisherman, passing along "contradictory" information calculated to direct the soldiers back towards enemy lines. Kerr felt satisfied that he had interviewed a sufficient number of witnesses. War was war.

At dusk Tuesday evening, May 28, B. J. M. Wright, a young reserve lieutenant was aboard the minesweeper HMS *Gossamer* as it swept at full speed into Dunkirk harbor. He found it "brilliantly lit by the fires from blazing oil tanks . . . the chimneys and buildings were silhouetted against the flames and the place looked like an inferno." He wasted no time in taking 450 men off the long pier, bringing the small craft down to its gunwales, and heading back out to sea.

About the same time, the destroyer *Wakeful* embarked almost 650 over capacity, and started for Dover via Kwinte Buoy, the long route. The *Wakeful* made the buoy—as did two German torpedo boats. Shortly after midnight, now Wednesday, May 29, one torpedo broke the *Wakeful*'s back and she sank in seconds. She carried with her most of the soldiers, who were below decks. Her captain, Commander Ralph Fisher, miraculously floated free.

Meanwhile, Wright, on the *Gossamer*, along the same route, would recall, "Out of the darkness came a strange noise like the cries of seagulls—and in a few seconds we found ourselves surrounded by men calling for help. It was impossible to leave these men drowning, although we knew there must be a submarine or MTB [motor torpedo boat] lurking in the neighborhood. We lowered our boats and started picking up survivors, but when a drifter appeared our captain called in our boats so that we could leave further rescue work to smaller ships."

The *Gossamer* continued for Dover. However, the destruction was not at an end. The drifter Wright had alluded to, the *Comfort* (which had rescued Commander Fisher), was joined by another, the *Nautilus*, the minesweeper *Lydd* and the destroyer *Grafton*. Shortly before 3:00 A.M., the *Grafton* was torpedoed by a submarine and also machine-gunned, killing her captain, Commander Charles Robinson, on the bridge.

Some thirty-five Army officers, sleeping in the wardroom, had been killed by the torpedo's explosion, directly beneath them.

The *Comfort* was raised in the air by the same explosion. In the confusion, thinking the drifter to be an enemy, gunners on the doomed *Grafton* opened fire, while the minesweeper *Lydd* rammed the *Comfort,* sinking her. Fisher went into the water again. The *Lydd,* the only survivor of the luckless group, headed for Dover, while other vessels arrived to search for those from the three sunken ships. Commander Fisher of the *Wakeful* was plucked from the waters a final time by the Norwegian freighter *Hird.* He was lucky. Most aboard the *Comfort,* including those from the *Wakeful,* were lost.

This Wednesday, Kerr found a much-needed water tank which had drifted ashore. Everyone was thirsty. Then he had a "brain wave to make a pier out of the lorries." It worked, to an extent, and for a limited distance. Sub-lieutenant J. K. Neale, aboard the minesweeper *Speedwell,* arrived to find "the beach black with troops, and aircraft were flying up and down bombing and machine-gunning them." He noticed a strange "pandemonium" caused by "loose horses galloping about the beach." Their presence—seemingly a leftover from World War I—remained unexplained.

Later in the afternoon the dive bombers concentrated on the long east pier or mole, the favored embarkation place other than the shallows themselves. A major target was the paddle steamer *Fenella,* whose crew transferred most of the stretcher cases to another paddler, the large *Crested Eagle,* newly arrived. While this operation was underway, the destroyer *Grenade,* on the other side of the narrow pier, was hit and started burning. A plucky trawler towed her away before she sank.

The *Crested Eagle,* with 1,000 on board, had steamed but several yards towards the harbor when she was struck by two bombs. Like the *Grenade,* she burst into flames. Although she was beached, upwards of 600 were killed. Paddle steamers suffered disproportionately this late Wednesday. Off La Panne, the *Gracie Fields* was hit. As she steamed helplessly in circles, minesweepers rescued most of the more than 750 troops aboard before she sank. The *Medway Queen,* luckier, was thumping back for a second load. Since it was now late evening and dark, her broad paddles churned up phosphorescent wakes. Twice, Luftwaffe planes homed in on the sparkling trail and dropped bombs "uncomfortably close."

Her crew was up to the challenge, and "devised oil bags which were lowered over the bow on either side just as they are used at sea to break the force of heavy waves," wrote John Graves. The tattletale wakes disappeared. However, the funnel now commenced to stream shiny sparks, the product of dirty pipes. A bucket chain was formed up against the funnel, ending with the tallest man aboard. At the price of many drenched backs, the watery expedient worked.

"The flotilla came under heavy fire from shore batteries, and some of the ships hauled out of the line as the sea spouted columns of water . . . the scene was awe-inspiring. Rows of great oil tanks were blazing furiously, and the glare was reflected on the clouds. Heavy shells plunged into the harbor . . . docks and quay walls were rubble, and torn and broken ships lay everywhere."

The young officer of the paddle steamer watched the soldiers as they "walked, stumbled or were carried" along the battered pier. "The gaps repaired by mess tables from ships, by ladders, wood planking and other materials taken from the debris around the harbor silhouetted by the flames [as] the weary file of men stumbled along its length."

As *Medway Queen* rode lower and lower in the water under the burden of her passengers, scaling ladders were placed against the pier down to her decks "as work went on to an accompaniment of rough oaths and crude instructions, hurrying and harrying . . . In the exhausted state of most of the soldiers it proved to be the right approach . . . Finally, when the old ship was down nearly to her sponsons [paddle wheel encasings] in the water, the word would come to the captain, "We are full up, sir, time we went!"

In London, the Railway Executive Committee was working on its own logistics: How to move the troops out of Dover once landed? Because the transport men had no idea of how many would actually be rescued, the problem was the knottier. Finally it was decided to adopt the most optimistic scenario: Most of the BEF and some of its allies would be evacuated. The four British railways were ordered to assemble nearly 200 trains. They would bypass London and follow primarily single-track lines to Dover. Since the Dover yards and station facilities were designed for moderate ferry service to Calais, it meant that the trains would be waiting on sidings extending back from the Kent coast scores of miles inland.

Ramsay, distressed at the losses of and damage to his ships, especially the destroyers, hurried some seven of the latter across the North Sea. Aboard one of them, the *Esk*, was Rear Admiral Frederick Wake-Walker, fifty-two, most recently captain of the battleship *Revenge*. As Captain Tennant was attempting to make sense out of the confusion on the beaches, Wake-Walker's assignment was "to try and get some organization into the embarkation" —that is, to get the men into the hundreds of craft, large and small, milling off the beaches.

As the *Esk* nosed into the chaotic French harbor in the first light of Thursday, May 30, another officer on the destroyer, Lieutenant Commander Cecil Wynne-Edwards, gazed upon "one of the most astounding and pathetic sights I have ever seen . . . the whole ten miles of beach was black from sand dunes to waterline with tens of thousands of men. In places they stood up to their knees and waists in water waiting for their turn to get into the pitiably few boats."

Wake-Walker's arrival was in keeping with the pandemonium of the moment. By plan, he transferred his flag to the minesweeper *Hebe*, only to change to the destroyer *Windsor* when the *Hebe* loaded up and started for Dover. Next, for obscure reasons, the admiral switched to Wright's *Gossamer,* and finally to two more ships, ending up on a torpedo boat, all in the space of a few hours, probably a record for transferral of command. Since he had lost his flag somewhere in the process, Wynne-Edwards later reported he now flew "a converted bath towel for we had no other."

There were also noncombatants on the beach with their own problems, including E. H. Phillips of the YMCA who was in charge of ten tea carts, loaded with cakes, sweets, cigarettes, and the like. In between passing out the refreshments to the cold and hungry troops, he joined them in ducking to the familiar warning: "Drop flat and stay still!" Most bombs exploded more or less harmlessly deep in the soft sand, but Phillips's entire rolling stock was destroyed when the building next to which they were parked was hit by incendiary shells.

Ted Harvey was now sailing on the 50-foot Thames River boat *Silver Queen.* He had shuttled all this Thursday morning to the *Esk,* carrying 100 soldiers each trip. When the destroyer herself steamed off, the young lieutenant in command of the *Silver Queen* decided he'd follow suit and take his passengers, largely French colonials, to Dover, via the short North Sea route "Z." Unfortunately, the route hugged the French coast. When a fog wisped in, the sailors lost their way. The mists lifted to reveal white cliffs. The Frenchmen waved their hats with joy. Suddenly, shells, "big as pint milk bottles," Harvey figured, slammed into the water around them. "Les Boche! Les Boche!" cried the soldiers. They were quite correct. The old river boat was right off the Calais breakwater, which was teeming with the enemy.

Luck was with the little vessel. The ack-ack (antiaircraft) cruiser *Calcutta* materialized from nowhere to return the shore fire quite effectively. She then shepherded the *Silver Queen* across the Channel, almost to Ramsgate. But the shelling had been too much for her weary hull; just as she was docking her seams opened up and she sank beneath the dark waters.

She wasn't the only casualty this May 30. The French destroyer *Bourrasque* struck a mine and was lost, with 150 of those on board. Three other destroyers were hit and at least nine smaller craft were sunk. It was almost impossible to keep tally on the fate of the small boats like the *Silver Queen*.

A ramp of lorries at Bray, similar to the one Tommie Kerr had devised, was expediting embarkations. Sergeant Giblett watched the continuing scene elsewhere: against the grim backdrop of "Dunkirk shattered and burning with the heavy pall of thick black smoke swirling over it. The massive queue of men noticeably moving forward . . . the mass of tired, hungry and thirsty men bunched together as they patiently moved forward nearer to where the ships were embarking as many as possible as quickly as circumstances permitted. The groans of wounded men on stretchers as stretcher bearers edged their way through towards the ships. Here some badly wounded men under the care of a nurse."

Past wrecked vehicles and damaged small boats the soldiers filed all evening in spite of bombing attacks, "during which flares were dropped by the planes and both the ships and men on the beachs were bombed and machine-gunned. As the planes droned overhead we would see a flicker of light and then a growing brightness as parachute flares dropped slowly towards the ground lighting up whole areas around the mole [pier] and the beaches. Then the planes swooped down to drop their bombs and machine-gun the area, causing a rapid dispersal of everyone towards any possible cover the ground afforded."

While Ramsay had the impression that matters were proceeding relatively smoothly, confusion nonetheless still reigned, with instances of traditional acrimony between officers and enlisted. For example, Corporal Edward Faulkes, a forty-four-year-old decorated veteran of World War I, recalled a captain telling him to "bugger off" since he was not of the officer's regiment. Faulkes replied by pushing his rifle into the captain's stomach, later noting:

> The small boats came in and discipline broke down. Everyone made a rush and soldiers pulled at one another in their haste to get into a boat. Finally, packed to capacity, their gunwales flush with the water, the boats were towed out to a waiting ship. I remember an officer telling me to pass the word that there must be no rushing of the rope ladders once we reached the ship's side. A man next to me shouted: "Sir, you can go and f--- yourself." The officer pretended not to hear.
>
> As we approached the ship—she was the destroyer *Scimitar*—I saw that the crew had lowered rope scrambling nets that stretched the length of her side. The officer shouted a hasty "one at a time!" then launched himself at the nets. That bastard was first out of the boat; he wasn't going to risk his skin any further. Then, without warning, our boat swamped and went down. I floundered along the destroyer's hull and somehow managed to grab the rope net. The next thing I knew was that a sailor was slipping a rope under my armpits and I was being hauled aboard. The only thought going through my mind was "Christ, I've lost my rifle—they'll stop nine quid out of my pay for that". *

Shortly after midnight the French *Siroco* was torpedoed by a Schnellboote off Kwinte Buoy. It appeared to her captain, Gui de Toulouse-Lautrec (who bore a lineal relationship to the painter) that he might save his destroyer, but a huge cloud of steam from the ruptured boilers attracted a Luftwaffe bomber, which dove to the attack. A magazine was hit, resulting in a shattering, brilliant explosion. A mere handful survived.

Friday, May 31, the sixth day of "Dynamo," Lieutenant

Dunkirk, by Robert Jackson.

Commander Wynne-Edwards was now aboard the 1,400-ton modern destroyer *Keith* with Admiral Wake-Walker. He observed that a "fresh northerly breeze and enough sea [made] inshore work difficult." Many boats beached at high tide had to await the next tide. "The sky was clear, but despite this enemy aircraft gave little trouble during the earlier part of the day," the lieutenant commander continued. "Our fighter patrols were entirely adequate until the late afternoon . . . bad weather and onshore wind, coupled with the stranding of so many small craft in the morning, slowed down the work on the beaches . . . it became evident there was no hope of bringing off the rearguard that night as had originally been planned."

Tommie Kerr, meanwhile, filled a whaler with "some straggling British troops." It was a hard row out to the larger ships, "even with a trained crew we barely made it. Twice the seas broke over us. The destroyers had all moved off towards Dunkirk and we pulled with tired locks out to sea . . . Presently up came, of all things, the Margate lifeboat and we climbed on board. We towed the whaler to the best of our judgment where it would float ashore to the others, and then let go."

More remarkable yet than the lifeboat was the *Massey Shaw*, a "float" of the London Fire Brigade. She arrived complete with pumps, hoses, and shining brass nozzles. She also brought much needed water. She had been listed simply in the catch-all class, "other vessels." The *Massey Shaw* embarked all she could and started for home, hoping her shallow draft would not cause her to be swamped. Although bombed and machine-gunned as she left the harbor, she escaped serious harm.

Before evening, destroyers such as *Keith* and *Hebe* found themselves ducking long-range artillery fire, while Wynne-Edwards recalled "a tremendous aerial battle . . . developing overhead. Our fighters were greatly outnumbered and while they engaged the enemy fighters many bombers broke through." He found most of the attacks "ill-executed," and at the *Keith*'s 31 knots she was able to twist and curve away from the missiles.

Sergeant Giblett, struggling onto the pier, watched the same aerial battle, filled with admiration for the "courage and determination" of the RAF in the face of formidable odds: "Planes darted about the sky twisting and weaving among the pattern of tracer bullets as machine guns rattled away. One plane disintegrated in a flash of flame and the pieces shattered as they fell to earth, while another dived down with its engine roaring and plunged into the sea with a mighty splash. [Aircraft losses in this battle were about thirty planes on each side.]

" . . . I was now at the beginning of the mole [pier], and started to make my way along it to where the cross-channel steamer seemed about to cast off, having taken on all the troops she could manage . . . suddenly a couple of German fighters dived steeply out of the sky and streaked towards the ship with their machine guns blazing away as they swept over the ships and across the mole. Instinctively, I threw myself flat and waited a few moments before having a quick glance to make sure they were not on the way back, then getting up I hurried towards the ship which seemed about to sail."

A naval officer standing near the ship shouted "Come on quick!" which inspired Giblett and a few others to race the remaining yards and jump on the ship, which was slowly leaving the pier. A few, curious to note, while abandoning their rifles, carried pet dogs in their arms.

None in the rescue fleet could satisfy the ravenings for food of the half-starved soldiers. "On every trip," noted Wright, aboard the *Gossamer*, "we found that the troops cleaned us out of food and the cooks were kept busy preparing stuff for them, as we felt their need was greater than ours—we kept going on cups of tea, bits of chocolate and ship's biscuit (which I always think taste of castor oil)." Cook Russell, on the *Medway Queen*, likened the men to "starving animals . . . pushing, shoving and shouting. Someone opened the starboard half-door and they started to flood for service right into the galley, then tried to exit from the other door . . . it was pandemonium."

Lord Gort and his large staff were returned to England on this same day, replaced by Major General Harold Alexander. At first he was put aboard the *Hebe*, then transferred to a motor torpedo boat. It was a wise decision since destroyers remained a prime target, one more being lost and six damaged this day.

Others were not as fortunate as Lord Gort. Those aboard the 30-foot yacht *Naiad Errant*, for example, had to row for several hours with makeshift paddles (fashioned from hatch covers) when the motor failed. But they made Dover.

On May 31 the evacuation peaked with more than 68,000 rescued, for a total of at least 196,000, or about two-thirds of the BEF. Now the British press was allowed to advise its readership of the dramatic operation. The prose became so ecstatic that Churchill felt compelled to warn his cabinet that "wars are not won by evacuations!"

"Thousands of the enemy are crossing the Channel under our very noses!" railed General Franz Halder, chief of staff of the Wehrmacht, "We do not want to have to fight them again." Yet Hitler would not order a resumption of the tank advance; in fact, he was about to activate his long-standing plans for turning the Panzers toward Paris. The Germans had failed to take the French capital in the last war. The Fuehrer did not want to miss this time. Desperate British and French rear unit action, employing such elite as the Grenadier and Cold Stream Guards, was maintaining the canal lines against Nazi ground troops. Marshal Goering's boast that his beloved Luftwaffe alone could trap and annihilate the Allies on the beaches was proving vacuous.

The *Gossamer*, with a charmed existence, continued in and out of "the inferno of Dunkirk." Wright, almost sleepless for five days, was convinced that there could be "no more unpleasant noise than when you know you are the target of a screaming dive bomber and very conspicuous." Wynne-Edwards, still aboard *Keith*, was of much the same mind as "Black Saturday," June 1, dawned.

After an all-night shelling as the German infantry advanced, the wreckage-strewn coast of La Panne appeared deserted. The troops were all pushing westward for Dunkirk, now the principal pocket for evacuation. Luftwaffe fighters and bombers met little opposition as the Allied ships ran short of ammunition.

"We in *Keith* had not a round remaining," wrote Wynne-Edwards. "In one attack on *Keith* about a dozen or more Junkers 87s dived vertically from about 10,000 feet and released their bombs at 2,000–3,000 feet. All missed, but one salvo dropped so close astern that it jammed the rudder." The ship steamed in tight circles "impotently" at 31 knots, unable to fight back.

Close by, the destroyer *Havant* and the minesweeper *Skipjack* were sunk, and the minesweeper *Salamander* seriously damaged. The destroyer, with 300 soldiers below deck, sank so quickly that almost none was saved. The railway steamer *Scotia* was hit and capsized with similar losses; the *Esk* rescued some.

Another railway steamer, the *Prague*, was crippled. The small gunboat *Mosquito* was set ablaze. Next, the French destroyer *Foudroyant*, also bombed, sank in minutes. A 500-pounder landed on the deck of the minesweeper *Brighton Queen*, killing some 300 French and Algerian troops. Damaged, the destroyer *Worcester* and minesweeper *Westward Ho* nonetheless struggled to Dover. The oily waters were filled with struggling men as smaller craft hastened to their rescue. Time ran out for *Keith*. After being hit amidships by one salvo, a single bomb hurtled down the aft funnel, exploding in the No. 2 boiler room. "The ship lost steam and had to anchor in the fairway," continued Wynne-Edwards. "After summoning two tugs to stand by *Keith*, the admiral [Wake-Walker] disembarked into a motor torpedo boat, and we proceeded towards Dunkirk to find out the situation inside the harbour. Attacks were still going on, and a squadron of dive bombers attacked the MTB as we steamed westwards."

The admiral and his staff were machine-gunned most of the way to shore. After the tugs had removed the remaining crew from the destroyer, she was sunk in a final attack. One of the tugs, however, the victim of a direct hit, disintegrated. There were no survivors.

Wake-Walker, unhappy with the way things were going, set off in the torpedo boat to report to Ramsay. Indeed, "Black Saturday" became blacker. Soon, another destroyer would be sunk along with several Channel steamers and vessels of similar size. Disembarking in Dover within the hour, Wynne-Edwards was greeted by his anxious wife, Bee Mary. "Oh, he was grimy, tired, unshaven," she recalled, "and wrapped in a blanket was a present—a little alcohol primus stove, the only thing he had salvaged."

Halfway across was the durable Ted Harvey, now on the 30-foot cabin cruiser *Thark*, one of several small craft under tow. She was down to her gunwales with 200 evacuees, including several French women. With little warning, the cable snapped, tipping the overloaded *Thark* onto her side and dumping her complement into the chilly North Sea. The tug picked up most, possibly all. This, sputtered one of the women, was indeed "Assez!"—quite enough. She had lost her whole family, and who did she have to blame? "Les Boche, Les Boche!"

Ramsay had reason to ponder if the cost were not too high. The casualties to the rescue fleet including auxiliaries had passed 25 percent and the rate continued to climb. The destroyers had suffered out of proportion: six sunk, twenty-three damaged, a casualty rate of 75 percent. This was intolerable. Even at Jutland in 1916 the Grand Fleet sustained but

10 percent losses, about the same as the German High Seas Fleet.

It was decided, for one measure, to discontinue the operation of the remaining destroyers off the French coast in daylight. Some ships, however, appeared indestructible, preeminent among them *Medway Queen*. On her deck a sort of "turret" of sandbags had been created. "On *Medway Queen*," Graves wrote, "we believed in concentration firepower. I took a party ashore at Dunkirk and succeeded in 'borrowing' a number of abandoned bren guns, these were lashed to stays and shrouds with a single turn of rope which formed an ideal swivel. Provided with a pile of ammunition beside each, they were handy for whoever was nearest to use in an attack.

"Beyond this, all troops and sailors who had a rifle were encouraged to blaze away at approaching aircraft on the sound principle that a storm of rifle fire could be as effective as a number of machine guns. The total result was impressive in discouraging any close approach by hostile aircraft and certainly contributed to . . . our good score of three low-flying aircraft shot down."

Among the *Queen*'s mixed passengers this trip was a group of Spanish sailors, refugees from the recent Spanish civil war, overtaken by the German advance. Leaving Dunkirk, the steamer was hailed by a uniformed officer in a small motor boat who urged that they proceed down the coast to a certain position where some troops were cut off and awaiting rescue. "Speaking by chance to the Spaniards," Graves recounted, "they were horrified and gave us to understand the place had been in German hands for two days. They had escaped from there!"

This was not a lone incident, as Ramsay himself knew. German agents had mingled with the rescue fleet to pass out false information. At the same time, in the early hours of Sunday, June 2, he was aware that "Dynamo" was reaching a climax. He ordered as large a concentration as possible of his fleet to attempt to lift before dawn "about 17,000 . . . probably in the proportion 50 percent British and 50 percent French."

The admiral was disturbed to learn that a number of small boats seemed to be cruising around empty off the French beaches. He radioed all large ships "to send them back to their duty on the coast."

Gossamer, on her fifth trip, poked through the wreckage offshore in the predawn Sunday smoke and darkness. "Decks were cluttered with empty shell cases," wrote Wright, "and, inside, the ship was like a shambles. Stench of stale wounds and sweat was enough to make the toughest stomach vomit." There also had been deaths aboard. Two, succumbing to their wounds, left the crew no alternative but "to tip them overboard." Wright, listening and peering through the night, had the feeling that "the troops had probably been captured and that the beach might be in the hands of the Germans. We knew that this was the very last lot of troops who had to be holding this village to protect Dunkirk.

"We could clearly see the fires of Dunkirk five miles away and hear the occasional boom of guns inland. About 0130 we heard a faint splashing noise in the water. Someone was swimming out to us.

"Presently there was a yell of 'Help! I'm finished! I've got an important message for your captain!' "

The best swimmer on board, who was a cook, jumped in and helped the exhausted swimmer onto the *Gossamer.* He turned out to be a Lieutenant Commander McClellan, from one of the sunken ships. He had kept afloat in spite of a bad shrapnel wound in the ankle. When he recovered his breath he gasped out a message that all ships eastward should be signaled to proceed to Dunkirk to which 6,000 British troops were converging.

"The scene as I saw it in the dim light," Wright continued, "with a circle of men standing silently round the two central figures, made me feel for the moment as though I was taking part in a Hollywood film.

"Soon the troops began to emerge and were standing in hundreds on the beach and in the water. They were yelling and shouting to us to fetch them off quickly and saying that there were many wounded. We could only yell back that we had no boats and that they must find some."

The larger troopships hove to offshore on Sunday morning and the little craft were assembled to chug in when darkness returned. In their number was Ted Harvey, now on his fourth boat, the *Hilfranoor.* Fighting off sleep and weariness as he surveyed the wreckage everywhere, he wondered if he was facing his last trip. The Germans must be on the outskirts of Dunkirk, he reasoned. They were not quite there yet, since French troops still held the perimeter. But without proper orders, much less leadership, their will to resist was necessarily weakening.

It was also past time to make a more concerted effort to evacuate the wounded. Captain Tennant had advised Ramsay: "Wounded situation acute and hospital ships should enter during day. Geneva Convention will be honourably observed, it is felt, and that the enemy will refrain from attacking." The hospital ship *Worthing* bravely steamed forth. Painted sparkling white, her hull and superstructure bore giant Red Cross emblems. They would be floodlighted in darkness. None could mistake her for a transport, much less a man o' war. But the Germans—the "Huns"—had historically ignored conventions, treaties, and so-called "rules of war." As it turned out, they would not change now. Two-thirds of the way across the North Sea, *Worthing* was attacked by a dozen Ju-88s. All bombs missed, but they were close enough to cause shock waves that put her engines out of line. She limped back for Dover.

Ramsay would try again. In late afternoon the hospital ship *Paris* started for Dunkirk. Perhaps the *Worthing* had been attacked by mistake? Churchill had expressed himself on the subject, concluding previously that hospital ships were "a special target of Nazi bombs."

Meanwhile, back at the beaches, Wynne-Edwards had something to say about the famed Grenadier Guards: "After three weeks of continuous fighting, [they came] marching in file down the pier, yes and some even singing as they marched, very different in hearing and discipline from the earlier thousands who had come off from the beaches. These were the real fighters, the heroes who defended Dunkirk to the last, who had borne the brunt of the fighting, and made all this outstanding evacuation possible."

He could never forget the dramatic spectacle "by night of the eastern arm of the harbor lit up in silhouette by the huge flames behind it with the never-ending stream of weary men moving down it, sometimes hurrying into a tired run, sometimes plodding blindly on towards safety, sometimes picked up stationary on the narrow parapet waiting for the next ship to berth."

Her Red Crosses brilliantly lit, the hospital ship *Paris* arrived after dark almost in sight of the beaches. Three Luftwaffe planes dropped bombs nearby. She was not hit but, like her predecessor, her steam pipes were ruptured. Distress rockets beckoned more enemy aircraft. An SOS brought several tugs which towed *Paris* to a buoy and evacuated her crew; there she sank. In an understatement, Ramsay reported, "The last attempt to evacuate the wounded by Hospital Carrier from Dunkirk was brought to naught."

More than 230 stretcher cases rested on the beach, with more arriving by the minute. Those who could barely hobble were making mighty efforts to leave their litters. The medical staff drew lots to see who would remain with the wounded. It fell to three doctors and thirty orderlies, but they did not have long to wait. Before midnight all were picked up by the surviving Channel steamers.

A few minutes past 3:00 A.M. Monday, June 3, Ramsay

received a message that all ships were hauling off while "the flow of French troops had dwindled away." One ship idled two and a half hours to embark her soldiers, so thin was the trickle waiting to board.

"No assurance could be obtained," the admiral added, "that this coming night would terminate the operation, and considerable anxiety was felt regarding the effect of the gradual exhaustion of officers and men of the ships taking part in the 'Dynamo.' This exhaustion was particularly marked in the Destroyer force, remnants of which had been executing a series of round trips without intermission for several days under navigation conditions of extreme difficulty and in the face of unparalleled air attacks."

In the predawn hours of Monday, Ramsay advised the Admiralty that continued operations would surely prove "beyond the limit of human endurance." He requested fresh forces if the evacuation were to continue. On his desk was a message from Captain Tennant, en route back with his staff aboard a torpedo boat: "Operation completed. Returning to Dover."

Well, almost, the admiral could think to himself, watching the familiar assorted shapes of big ships and little boats poking towards the Dover breakwater through the morning mists. He had seen others during the night steaming the other way, including the *Medway Queen*. Her seventh crossing, it probably set a record, but records, superlatives, and the impossible, had become the rule, not the exception, in the illogic of war.

The Times of London, this June 3, was headlining "Bulk of the B.E.F. Saved." It was close to the truth. "The sands were running out very fast," according to Graves aboard the *Medway Queen*. "We took on board about 400 French troops. Shelling in the harbor was very heavy. A destroyer astern was hit and flung forward against our starboard paddle box, extensively damaging the sponson." Nonetheless, the paddle steamer waited into the afternoon for any stragglers even though the captain was in receipt of an order from Ramsay that all ships were to leave Dunkirk by 2:30 the next morning, Tuesday, June 4. He had made this decision in the face of intelligence estimating about 30,000 soldiers still near the French and Belgian beaches.

Monday night, advance German troops entered the outskirts of Dunkirk. The *Medway Queen* did not cast off until 1:00 A.M. Tuesday, with one of her officers "strumming a mandolin on the after deck to cheer up the tired Frenchmen." Visible now were the dark silhouettes of enemy soldiers running along the pier. Bullets rattled off the paddle steamer's sides.

With her were the destroyers *Express* and *Shikari*. The latter, a World War I relic, bore not one scar from her week's evacuation. The trio thus became the last major vessels to leave Dunkirk. There was one final casualty, the block ship *Gourko*, which struck a mine before she could fulfill her intended mission, that of being scuttled to obstruct a channel to the enemy. A fog rolled in as the three steamed into the North Sea. The machine-gunning faded, the light from the fires on shore dimmed into a glow.

About 12 hours later, at 2:30 P.M. Tuesday, "Dynamo" was formally terminated. At 3:00 P.M. Winston Churchill went before the House of Commons to review the historical nine day operation. Warning that "we must be very careful not to assign to this deliverance the attributes of a victory," he continued:

> Even though large tracts of Europe and many old and famous States have fallen or may fall into the grip of the Gestapo and all the odious apparatus of Nazi rule, we shall not flag or fail. We shall go on to the end, we shall fight in France, we shall fight in the seas and oceans, we shall fight with growing confidence and growing strength in the air, we shall defend our island, whatever the cost may be, we shall fight on the beaches, we shall fight on the landing-grounds, we shall fight in the fields

> and in the streets, we shall fight in the hills; we shall never surrender, and even if, which I do not for a moment believe, this island or a large part of it were subjugated and starving, then our Empire beyond the seas, armed and guarded by the British Fleet would carry on the struggle, until, in God's good time, the New World, with all its power and might, steps forth to the rescue and the liberation of the Old.

As the radio commentator Edward R. Murrow put it, Churchill was demonstrating his ability "to mobilize the English language and send it into battle."

Just under 339,000 troops, about two-thirds British, had been rescued. Some 2,000 had died during the operation. Of the civilian ship crews, 126 had been killed or drowned. The RAF lost 80 pilots, the Luftwaffe somewhat more. Each side lost between 130 and 140 aircraft.

Curiously, the Royal Navy never released figures on human losses, although thirty-five of the major vessels were sunk and forty-one damaged. As a class, the destroyers suffered the worst, with nine lost. Almost all of the complement of *Wakeful* —150—went down with her. Other major ships included minesweepers, sloops, gunboats, trawlers, personnel carriers, ferries and others. Admiral Ramsay himself did not know the exact size of the evacuation fleet, although estimates ranged as high as 845 vessels, with a staggering "little ships" casualty rate of more than 25 percent.

All equipment was abandoned: guns, large and small, and almost 65,000 vehicles, which included tanks. But much of this was obsolete, of the last war's vintage, which would and should have been replaced.

"Deliverance," as Churchill described the evacuation, was made possible through "valour, by perseverance, by perfect discipline, by dauntless service, by resources, by skill, by unconquerable fidelity." David Divine, a correspondent who was there, tended to agree with his prime minister, pointing to "the naval organization once it got underway." In conversations with this author, he elaborated on the navy's ability tosweep channels as well as to divert traffic to different channels. He alluded as well to the often paralyzing rivalry between Nazi land, sea, and air forces.

Admiral Ramsay, disappointed at the "extremely disheartening" RAF cover, paid tribute to "a continued flow in ever increasing numbers of small power boats and beach craft," insuring "a continued evacuation from the beaches." Wynne-Edwards was among many naval officers who "felt most of the time we wouldn't complete it." He thought it "little less than a miracle that the five-foot wide wooden pathway along which so many tens of thousands walked to safety should have remained intact to the end." Ted Harvey was convinced the Germans underestimated their foe, typified by a remark attributed to one of their generals, "What are the stupid British up to?"

The weather and especially the calm seas surely played a role in the miracle. The religious-minded found the only plausible answer in the intervention of Divine Providence. That Hitler deliberately halted his tanks in the hopes of a negotiated peace with Great Britain does not bear hard scutiny. The heavy losses in the evacuation fleet and on the beaches scarcely lends evidence of any beneficence from the Reich Chancellery.

The Low Countries, with their dikes and canals, were considerably less than ideal for tanks. The Wehrmacht's lines were overextended, and nearly 50 percent of all the German motorized equipment was said to be in need of maintenance. Besides, to the Nazis the BEF appeared already beaten. Hitler had apparently believed the wily Goering's boast that his Luftwaffe alone could take care of the foe. Mostly, perhaps, the Reich's dictator wanted the swastika to fly over Paris, and that it did ten days after the fall of Dunkirk, on June 14.

Intoxicated with his easy victories, the Fuehrer ignored two elements that would prove mortal: a "delivered" army that returned refreshed, rearmed, and regrouped and, as Churchill had predicted, the New World with all its power and might [stepping] forth to the rescue and the liberation of the Old."

Once again, ships, in both a unique and dramatic fashion, had reshaped the course of history.

Postscript: Admiral Ramsay did not survive to witness the final defeat of Nazi Germany. He died in an airplane accident in September 1944 en route to the ill-starred "Market Garden" plan to capture bridges at Arnhem, Holland and nearby and thus turn the Siegfried Line.

Admiral Wake-Walker, commanding the heavy cruisers *Suffolk* and *Norfolk,* the following May took part in the pursuit and destruction of the German battleship *Bismarck.*

Captain William Tennant's luck held. On December 10, 1944 he survived the sinking of HMS *Repulse,* of which he was commander, off Malaya. Along with a companion battleship, the magnificent new *Prince of Wales,* she had been bombed by Japanese planes in a demonstration of airpower against unescorted capital warships. (See Chapter Three) Cecil Wynne-Edwards, retired as a captain, was living on a lovely farm on Hayling Island, near Portsmouth, so far as the author knows, and where he was entertained. And John Douglas Graves, of *Medway Queen,* was a "marine and cargo surveyor" in Liverpool when last this author spoke with him.

Chapter Six

USS *Arizona*

It was an hour and a half after sunrise over Hawaii and not quite eight o'clock Sunday morning, December 7, 1941, when the many naval vessels in Pearl Harbor slowly began to come to life. A leisurely pace after traditional Saturday nights at Navy stations had long been the unofficial order of the day.

Aboard the flagship of Battleship Division One, USS *Arizona*, newly out of drydock, Milton Thomas Hurst, an aviation machinist's mate third class, was on the quarterdeck—an aft area of a ship reserved in the old Navy for officers—basking in the brilliant sunshine, smoking a cigarette.

"The first bit of excitement I noticed," he would write, "was that the Officer-of-the-deck [OOD] and Junior OD were standing near the Admiral's gangway, they were pointing and looking west towards Ford Island. Out of curiosity I went over to the lifeline to see what everyone was looking at. I saw a large column of smoke going up into the air.

"At this time the OOD told the boatswain's mate of the watch to sound general alarm, which he did on the double . . . I thought there was a fire on one of the ships, or on the Air Station so I went up into #5 casemate to see what was going on.

"It was now that the first word was said about an air attack and then everyone seemed to think it was the Army having a mock attack. I watched several planes sweep over Ford Island

and one went over our fantail and I saw the red spot on the wing.

"Our guns then opened up and it first struck me we were being attacked."

The story of that day, however, and especially of the *Arizona*, goes back in time, certainly to October 1916 when the 31,400-ton battleship went into commission. Exceeded in size only by the *Pennsylvania* and the *New Mexico*, she honored that southwestern state whose name had been derived from the Spanish-Indian "Arizonac" meaning, it is believed, "few springs." Arizona had been admitted to the Union only four years before in 1912.

The new warship's length was 608 feet, or about 100 feet less than the *Great Eastern*'s. Her beam was 97 feet, and main armament twelve 14-inch guns. Upon America's entry into World War I, the handsome battleship was based at Norfolk for use in gunnery training. That her fuel was bunker oil had kept the *Arizona* out of the European conflict since the British navy stoked her men o' war with coal. After the Armistice, she steamed for Portland, England, to operate briefly with the British Grand Fleet. In December she was part of the honor escort for the transport *George Washington*, which took President Wilson to the Paris Peace Conference aimed at creating the ill-starred League of Nations.

She carried 238 doughboys on her homeward voyage. During the ensuing two years she helped protect American lives during Greek-Turkish disturbances and was present at the historic air bombings of old German warships off Cape Charles, June–July 1921. It proved a dark omen of the future.

In the 1920s, while *Arizona* participated in maneuvers off both coasts, international naval conferences were being held which would shape not only the battleship's destiny but that of the entire world. In sum, Japan remained dissatisfied with the capital ships ratio Great Britain, the United States and France sought to impose on her. While these powers agreed to scrap a number of ships and cease construction on others, Japan tore up blueprints. She ultimately withdrew from all naval limitations conferences (in 1935) when denied parity with the United States and Great Britain. Tokyo's refusal to limit the size of major warships to 35,000 tons was the signal for the other signatories to the ill-starred conferences to launch all-out naval rearmament programs.

In the 1930s, Japan was doing more than expanding her navy. Her armies were running amok in China and Manchuria. On the Yangtze, her bombers sank the U.S. gunboat *Panay* December 12, 1937. Yet, in the face of her naked aggression and the obvious truth that her warlords were in control, the West continued to supply Japan with the raw materials for war, especially scrap metal and gasoline. (When trolleys were being replaced by buses, the author, as a boy, recalls the old tracks near his home in suburban Maryland (outside of Washington, D.C.) being torn up and shipped off. His father observed laconically that they were surely on their way to Japan.)

By 1938, the Japanese had captured all of China's major ports and declared a "New Order for East Asia," a so-called "co-prosperity sphere." Those who did not care to "cooperate" would soon be liquidated if they had not been already. Much of the Far East was proclaimed off-limits to Westerners.

USS *Arizona*, meanwhile, entered the 1930s fully modernized. Gone were the World War I vintage cage masts, now replaced with tripods. New 5-inch guns bristled where her old 3-inch antiaircraft battery had fired. Additional armor plate in the form of "blisters" was added at waterline as a protection against torpedoes (although this would turn out to be a futile effort).

In September 1938 Rear Admiral Chester W. Nimitz hoisted his pennant aboard the *Arizona* as the flagship of Battleship Division One. Two years later she joined the fleet at Pearl Harbor, the presence of which was aimed at deterring further

Japanese encroachments in the Pacific. The commander of the Pacific Fleet, Admiral James O. Richardson, wasn't pleased. He called the Hawaiian anchorage no less than a "mousetrap."

In 1941, a former captain of the battleship, Admiral Isaac C. Kidd, Annapolis Class of 1906 (where he was known as "Cap,") assumed command of Battleship Division One. Captain Franklin van Valkenburgh became the skipper of the *Arizona.*

While the Pacific Fleet waited, uselessly it would turn out, at Pearl Harbor, largely clustered about Ford Island, American-Japanese relations deteriorated. In July 1941, the United States, in concert with England, froze all Japanese assets and embargoed such strategic raw materials as oil, iron ore, maganese, and scrap. Tokyo's answer that fateful autumn was to launch peace talks with Washington while hastening preparations for war.

In mid-November, the new premier, Lieutenant General Hideki Tojo, a descendant of two generations of samurai warriors and known appropriately as "razor blade," dispatched a second envoy, Saburo Kurusu to confer with Secretary of State Cordell Hull. Tough and devious, he had signed the Tripartite Pact as ambassador to Berlin. Kurusu would supplement the mission of Admiral Kichisaburo Nomura, ambassador to Washington. The mild-mannered Nomura was considered a friend of the West and advocate of peace.

On November 23, a Ten-Point Note was sent from the U.S. State Department to Tokyo aimed at a nonaggression pact between Japan and other powers with interests in the Pacific. As a condition for having its assets unfrozen and embargoes lifted, Japan would withdraw from occupied lands, including French Indochina. On that very date, however, a powerful task force built around six aircraft carriers sailed from the Kuriles on a course for Hawaii. It had been hand-tailored by the ranking admiral of the Japanese Imperial Fleet, Isoroku Yamamoto for one purpose and one alone: to destroy the U.S. fleet at

Pearl Harbor. (He would later confide to a very few that as he did so, he was mindful of the "terrible resolve" of the American people and knew Japan must win the war in no more than six months or face annihilation.)

U.S. Naval Intelligence became aware in the immediately ensuing days that something was amiss because of the sudden and total absence of radio transmission from these carriers and other major ships of the task force. In fact, Lieutenant Commander Edwin T. Layton, intelligence officer of the Pacific Fleet, would confide this information to the new fleet commander, Admiral Husband E. Kimmel. After thinking about this information a few moments, the admiral asked in amazement, "Do you mean to say they could be rounding Diamond Head and you wouldn't know it?"

Kimmel was equally perplexed by a message from the Chief of Naval Operations, Admiral Harold R. Stark, which inadvertently alluded to a "purple machine." Neither Layton nor anyone else in Hawaii knew what this was, and for good reason. The armed forces in this highly critical area had not been supplied with one. (Yet General Douglas MacArthur, commanding U.S. Army Forces in the Far East, had been favored with this vital piece of equipment.)

For more than a year the Army and Navy had been breaking the Japanese diplomatic code by use of a wondrous deciphering machine arbitrarily tagged "purple." The term "magic" was applied to the eavesdropping process itself. In recent weeks, the messages had accelerated both in volume and significance. For example, the Japanese consulate in Honolulu was asked for more and more details about the Pearl Harbor anchorage also about the number and types of warships there. Finally, to the Japanese embassy in Washington a telltale "circular" was sent including the code warning, "In case of Japan-U.S. relations in danger, 'east wind rain.'" It would become known as the "winds message."

On December 3, Japanese diplomats in Hong Kong,

Singapore, Batavia, Manila, Washington, and London were ordered to "destroy most . . . codes and ciphers at once and to burn all other important and confidential secret documents."

Early Saturday morning, December 6, a new dispatch from the Tokyo Foreign Office to Ambassador Nomura was decoded by the Army and Navy: "This separate message is a very long one. I will send it in 14 parts and I imagine you will receive it tomorrow . . . I want you to please keep it secret for the time being." It proved, as it tapped in, hour after hour, to be indeed "very long." Rambling and verbose, it reaffirmed "the immutable policy of the Japanese government to insure the stability of East Asia," denounced the "American government obsessed with its own views and opinions," rejected the Ten Point Note out of hand, and closed the door to future negotiations.

The message, foreshadowing a break in diplomatic relations, bothered Army and Navy intelligence officers far more than their ranking superiors to whom they showed it Saturday evening. The consensus seemed to be that it was just another "diplomatic paper" with "little military significance." An exception was President Roosevelt, who was quoted as observing, rather flatly, "This means war."

In Pearl Harbor, it was a quiet Saturday, marked by minor comings and goings of smaller vessels and liberty launches. Shortly before 10:00 A.M. the repair ship *Vestal* warped alongside the *Arizona*. Her captain, Commander Cassin B. "Ted" Young, paid his respects to Admiral Kidd and Captain van Valkenburgh. The engineering officers of the two ships conferred on the repair work to be done. That evening, the high point was to be the "Battle of the Bands" in the Naval Receiving Station. The largest entrants were from the eight battleships present.

One Army officer, however, was in no mood for relaxation or any sort of entertainment that Saturday evening: Lieutenant Colonel George W. Bicknell, assistant G2 (intelligence officer) to Lieutenant General Walter C. Short, commander of the Army's Hawaiian Department. He was deeply disturbed by the transcript of a long telephone conversation with a Tokyo newspaper given to him by the Honolulu FBI agent, Robert Shivers. The telephone of Mrs. Motokazu Mori, the wife of a local dentist and listed as a correspondent for the *Yomiuri Shimbun*, had long been tapped.

She had discussed many topics including the fleet, airplanes observed, the number of sailors in town, civilian workers, factories, searchlights, possible plans to evacuate the Japanese population, the weather, and a great deal of talk about specific flowers, which Bicknell believed to be a code. The intelligence officer hastened to Fort Shafter through streets filled with Christmas shoppers, spectators returning from a football game, and the Saturday night press of soldiers and sailors out on the town.

At "brass row" Bicknell found General Short in his whites, preparing to go to dinner at Schofield Barracks. Obviously impatient to get started, Short, together with his intelligence officer Lieutenant Colonel Kendall Fielder, glanced through the Mori message, then observed to Bicknell that he might be "a little too intelligence conscious." The general bade the latter goodnight and was on his way.

Pondering the message, Bicknell scarcely slept that night. His counterparts in Washington felt the same, for one, among them Colonel Rufus S. Bratton, chief of the Army's Far Eastern Section in G2. Early Sunday morning "magic" had produced urgent instructions from Tokyo to Nomura specifying that the Fourteen Part Message be delivered at precisely 1:00 P.M. Washington time.

"I tried to figure out where it would be dawn when it was one o'clock in Washington," Bratton would recall. He guessed it would be 7:30 in Hawaii, though actually it would be 6:26 this Sunday morning. The colonel was aware of Japan's history for attacking without warning in the early hours of morning. He knew he must find the Chief of Staff, General George C. Marshall, and advise him of the latest message and of his fears.

But time had already run out. The "missing" carriers, part of a formidable Japanese task force, were already nearing launch point approximately 275 miles north of Pearl Harbor. A total of 183 planes—torpedo-bombers, high-level bombers, dive bombers, and fighters—were warming up their engines.

At 3:50 A.M, patrolling the entrance to Pearl Harbor, the World War I four-stack destroyer *Ward* received a blinker message from the minesweeper *Condor* that an object resembling a periscope had been sighted. Not until 6:45 A.M was the conning tower of a small submarine actually seen. The *Ward* opened fire and dropped depth charges. Oil and debris indicated the intruder had been sunk.

"We have attacked, fired upon and dropped depth charges upon submarine operating in defensive area," the destroyer advised the Fourteenth Naval District at 6:50 A.M. The spoken radio message was also heard by the communications watches on the ships in Pearl Harbor. None went to battle stations.

A few minutes later, about 7:02 A.M, two Signal Corps privates, Joseph Lockard and George Elliott, working on experimental radar on Kahuku Point at Oahu's northernmost tip, noticed a sudden "shower of blips" on the screen. It indicated a large flight of aircraft some 132 miles to the north. They phoned their watch officer, Lieutenant Kermit A. Tyler, at Fort Shafter.

Knowing that a flight of B-17s was due in from the West Coast and placing but little confidence in the new electronic gadget, Tyler responded, "Don't worry about it." In fact, Station KGMB, instead of signing off at midnight after its usual "Night Owl" program, had kept on spinning records as an aid to the bombers' navigation, at the Army's request. Nonetheless, the two privates watched the nearing images on the bright circular screen until 7:15 when the truck arrived to take them to breakfast. They switched off the radar.

Although the vanguard of the hostile aircraft was spotted over various points of the island, including airfields and barracks, a few minutes before 8:00 A.M and mistaken for Army or Navy planes on early morning maneuvers, Rear Admiral William R. Furlong aboard his flagship, the old minelayer *Oglala,* was perhaps the first to recognize the red ball beneath the wings of the attackers and its significance. He ordered the signal hoisted: "All ships in harbor sortie!"

Next, Pacific Fleet Headquarters broadcast: "All ships in the Hawaiian area . . . air raid on Pearl Harbor! This is no drill!" The transmission was picked up by an alert radioman at the Mare Island Navy Station, San Francisco, and relayed at once to Washington. President Roosevelt was informed about 1:40 P.M. even as the Japanese envoys were en route to the State Department to deliver the Fourteen-Point Message, the contents of which were already known.

"Battleship row" became the target for the torpedo bombers' major attack. Zooming in 40 to 50 feet above the water, they made an initial run on the *Arizona.*

Ensign George B. Lennig, a Naval Reservist, was asleep in his quarters "located in the lower ward room about eight frames aft of the athwartships armored bulkhead on the third deck. I awakened upon the passing of the word, 'All hands man your general quarters stations!' and had commenced dressing when I heard a violent explosion somewhere forward. The lights went out on both the normal lighting circuit and the battle circuit.

"I completed dressing and started forward and up the ladder to the second deck when a very close and violent explosion sent flame and burning debris down the ladder. After falling back for a moment, I ascended to the second deck and found the smoke and fire, caused by a bomb hit outside the captain's cabin, too dense to pass through. I went to the foot of the ladder and connected the fire hose, but there was no pressure. This failing, I soaked a towel in the waste water bucket under the basin in my room and proceeded up and forward to find that the oil-covered water was now rushing into the second deck from what appeared to be forward. I attempted to drop the hatch to the lower ward room country but was able to loosen only one supporting bar."

Ensign Jim D. Miller felt one explosion, followed by two more: "I still did not realize that there was actually an air raid. As soon as I came up to the second deck from the lower wardroom, I met a gunner's mate who said he was trying to find the magazine keys. I went into the captain's cabin to call him and get the keys if possible. The captain was not there. I then looked in the gunnery officer's stateroom to see if I could get the keys from him, but he was not in either. By that time the gunner's mate had left me, and I went on down to the third deck.

"General quarters was sounded. I went into Turret III through the lower handling room to the booth, took the turret officer's station and manned the 2JE phones to plot. Communications to plot were OK. However, Turret III was the only turret I heard on the line. Shortly after I had reached the booth the turret was shaken by a bomb explosion of not very great intensity. After a minute or two a much more terrific explosion shook the turret. Smoke poured in through the overhang hatch, and I could see nothing but reddish flame outside. The 2JE phones went dead, all power went off the turret, and all lights went out.

"From all reports that I could get from inside the turret, the turret was not even half manned. I believe that it was at about this time that a bomb hit on the starboard side of the quarterdeck next to Turret IV, penetrated down to the third deck and exploded. (From later examination I found that this bomb had glanced off the side of Turret IV and then had penetrated the decks.) My lower handling room crew was shaken up, and water began coming into the lower handling room. Explosion gases were filling the turret from the overhang hatch and from openings into the lower room. I stepped outside the turret to see what the condition was on the quarterdeck. There were several small fires on the deck and awnings. I notice several badly burned men lying on deck.

"I figured that with the turret not completely manned, with all power off, and with the turret full of suffocating gas we could do nothing toward repelling the attack. I sent the word into the turret for all hands to come outside and fight fires. All hands came out.

"I found all fire hoses already connected to plugs on the quarterdeck, but there was no water on the fire mains. An attempt to call the center engine room on the ship's service telephone was unsuccessful because the telephones were out of commission. It was also impossible to reach the engine room because of fire and smoke and gas. The first lieutenant was on the quarterdeck and in charge. About all we could do was to try to put out fires and drag some of the wounded men under the protection of the overhangs of the turrets. We put out several of the small fires— papers and awnings on deck— with buckets of water. Fuel oil was coming up from some place on the port side and was catching on fire.

"The quarterdeck began to become awash starting at the break of the deck at frame 88. The main and forecastle decks forward of frame 88 were ablaze. Oil on top of the water was feeding the fire. At one time the first lieutenant asked me if I had seen the captain or the admiral. I told him I had been in the captain's cabin and had not seen him. He wanted me to go down into the cabin and check again. White, T. A., BM2c, [boatswain's mate second class] and myself went down into the cabin, looked around, felt in the captain's bed, but could find no trace of him. However, it was dark and the smoke was bad, and it is possible that we could have missed him.

Nevertheless, I am sure he was not there. We did not go into the admiral's cabin. We came back up to the quarterdeck."

E. L. Wentzlaff, an aviation ordnance machinist second class, heard "a whining sound, followed by a tremendous explosion that caused the ship to virtually rise out of the water, shudder and start settling down by the bow." (An armor-piercing bomb had detonated in the forward powder magazine.)

Two men manning a fire hose, but without pressure, were simply "carried away," then "men came pouring out from the direction of the Marine compartment, terribly burned, shocked, and shrapnel wounded. Many went over the side into the water, as the terrific flames from burning oil and the explosion itself greedily licked a patch across the quarterdeck."

Wentzlaff ran down the admiral's gangway, swam to the latter's barge, cut it loose and "proceeded to make the crew's gangway. It was settling so fast and debris, smoke and cowardly strafing of the Japs made it difficult progress; after finally making the gangway we again boarded the ship and began carrying wounded, shocked and grotesquely burned shipmates and officers off."

Chief Turret Captain George K. Campbell hurried to the lower ammunition handling room of Turret IV, his station, just before the lights flashed off "and everything was pitch dark." He continued: "I ordered everybody from the lower room up into the turret. My division officer was not there, so I had to take immediate charge. About that time, E. H. Pecotte, [a gunner's mate second class] showed up with a flashlight and we got up into the turret chamber.

"Gas then began to become evident in the turret, and the men couldn't breathe very well. This gas was apparently from the storage batteries, and was leaking through around the sprung water-tight door. Pecotte discovered the source of this odor and immediately pulled off his dungaree shirt and trousers and stuffed them around the edges of the door where the odor was coming from. This did not clear the turret of gases, but it did stop the supply, and helped considerably. Water was rising rapidly and it was already up to the pointer group. I then sent Pecotte outside on deck to see if it was safe to leave the turret and have the men all leave.

"When Pecotte came back into the turret he reported that he had asked Lieutenant Commander S. G. Fuqua [the damage control officer] if the ship was being abandoned, and was told that it was, so I ordered all hands out on deck. We stayed under the overhang of the turret for about fifteen minutes. In the meantime I ordered three men to cut life rafts down and put them over the side aft and secure them to the lifeline. Pecotte then took a flashlight and said he was going back in the turret to make sure that everyone was out of the turret.

"Under the overhang, just as he started back in the turret, he met Peil, W. J., BM2c, coming out of the turret. Peil stated that he had been crawling around and feeling for anyone left in the turret, and that he did not believe anyone was left. However, Pecotte completed his inspection of the turret and returned stating that he had found no one inside the turret. Pecotte and Peil then began picking up wounded men and removing them to the overhang of the turrets and later to the boats for transportation to the hospital and the [hospital ship] *Solace*. This they were doing under the supervision of Commander Fuqua who had complete charge of the quarterdeck.

"A man on deck of the *Vestal* [still warped beside the *Arizona*] called for someone to throw off their lines." But this had already been done. The repair ship herself had sustained considerable damage.

Ensign D. Hein was possibly the last to observe Admiral Kidd and Captain Van Valkenburgh alive. He wrote: "I saw the admiral on the signal bridge. Then I went up to the navigation bridge. The only people up there were the captain, the quartermaster and myself. The quartermaster asked the captain if he wanted to go into the conning tower but the captain did not want to, making phone calls. [The conning tower would remain relatively unscathed.]

"Suddenly, the whole bridge shook like it was in an earthquake, flames came through the bridge windows which had been broken by gunfire. We three were trying to get out the port door at the after end of the bridge during all this shaking, but could not. We staggered to the starboard side and fell on the deck just forward of the wheel, finally I raised my head and turned it and saw that the port door was open.

"I got up and ran to it, and ran down the port ladders, passing through flames and smoke. Then I climbed halfway down the signal bridge ladder and had to jump to the boat deck as it was bent way under. Then I climbed down a hand railing to the galley deck. The flames and smoke on the boat deck and galley deck were decreasing in intensity . . . I walked aft and down the ladder to the port quarterdeck.

"Then I walked to the other side and down the officers' ladder to the barge."

Somewhere along Ensign Hein's escape route, Captain Van Valkenburgh apparently was lost.

Ensign Lennig "heard an intermittent screaming from the captain's cabin and swam in there and brought out a mess attendant who had been badly injured. Another mess attendant joined me from some place and with the water almost reaching the overhead, I emerged with the wounded mess attendant to the quarterdeck where I met Commander Fuqua, who gave the command, 'All hands abandon ship!', after all wounded men were put into the boats that were alongside the starboard quarterdeck. An oil fire was burning from about frame 110 forward in flames forty to fifty feet in height."

Martin Bruns, a yeoman second class, had been in the gunnery office, preparing to sell newspapers, as was his custom on Sundays, when "a deep rumbling sound was heard, coming from up forward . . . accompanied by a slight tremor of the ship. It was similar to the noise caused when a hatch is let fall. I looked out of the port and saw part of the Marine guard coming forward on the double. When they came to the break of the quarterdeck several went up the ladder to the boat deck.

"After leaving the gunnery office I went into the Marine compartment to sell papers as I still did not know what the cause was of all these occurring incidents. There was indistinct babbling but no loud noises. From here I could get a good view to the outside through the double doors on the starboard side. . . ."

When a shipmate called to him that the minesweeper *Oglala* had been bombed and "that the enemy was strafing our men on topside this convinced me definitely. I turned to the gunnery office and then heard the air raid alarm. After opening the door and seeing the men inside I could tell that they were on their way to man their battle stations. They stopped me and inquired what it was really all about for no one deemed it possible what was happening."

He then joined a group fighting a fire in the executive officer's office.

"The closest fire hose and fire plug were in the Marine compartment. This was not suitable at that instance as too much traffic was going. The fire hose was moved out to the fire plug forward of barbette #3. It was connected and the water turned on. Too many kinks in the hose prevented water passing through so the water was turned off and the hose straightened. Although the fire was to port of us the fire hose was led out to starboard since a fire had originated in the vicinity of the optical work shop. . . .

"After the water failed and almost immediately thereafter the small cargo hatch forward of #3 deck winch seemed to explode. The force of the explosion pressed me against the barbette and I am uncertain how long I was in this state for when I moved and glanced around the quarterdeck many of the others previously on the quarterdeck were no longer to be seen.

"Two men were lying by the exhaust blower, on their backs. These two men came to after I slapped them a couple of times and they undoubtedly were stunned by the explosion for they got up and moved about. I did not recognize either of them.

"The forward part of the ship was not visible due to smoke and fire.

"Wentzlaff then called to me that we were to abandon ship. My trip to the life line was very unsteady as the ship seemed to be pitching. The water was covered with fuel oil.

"After going into the water to swim to the beach as my first thought ran, I was attracted by calls for help from several swimmers. First I kicked off my shoes and then helped those calling for help. Other ablebodied men were giving help also to those which could not swim because of wounds, burns, and their poor eyesight. These men were taken to the after quay to which the *Arizona* was moored.

"Before leaving the ship Mr. Fuqua was seen directing groups of men. Several officers were also seen but I could not tell who they were. Mr. Fuqua was facing forward and standing about in the middle of the quarterdeck aft of the staff gangway."

Commander Fuqua, the damage control officer who had become the senior officer present, was singled out for praise by a number of those surviving. One was Donald A. Graham, a machinist's mate first class who, like others, was frustrated by the lack of water in the hoses. While struggling to obtain pressure the forward magazine blew up and he was conscious of an "awful 'swish' and hot air blew out of the compartments . . . Yellowish smoke was pouring out of the hatches from below decks.

"There was lots of men coming out on the quarterdeck with every stitch of clothing and shoes blown off, painfully burned and shocked. Mr. Fuqua set an example for the men in being unperturbed, calm, cool and collected, exemplifying the courage and traditions of an officer under fire. It seemed like the men painfully burned, shocked and dazed, became inspired and took things in stride, seeing Mr. Fuqua so unconcerned about the bombing and strafing . . . as there was no 'going to pieces' or 'growing panicy' noticeable and he directed the moving of the wounded and burned men who were on the quarterdeck to the motor launches and boats. He gave orders to get the life rafts on #3 barbette down, supervised the loading of the wounded and burned casualties, assisted by Ensign J. D. Miller, who set a very good example for a younger officer in being cool. . . .

"The signal gang, quartermasters and all hands on the bridge went up; as the signalmen were trying to put out a fire in the signal rack and grabbing signal flags out to hoist a signal, the whole bridge went up, flames enveloped and obscuring them from view as the flames shot upward twice as high as the tops. A bomb hit on the starboard side of the after 5-inch guns and antiaircraft guns and got most of the Marine crew and antiaircraft crews. It seemed as though one bomb hit the port after antiaircraft crew and came down through the casemate and executive officer's offices. The whole port compartment . . . was a flaming inferno and the ship settled rapidly from forward aft.

"The wardroom, portside, was flooded even with the bottom of the deck coamings and yellowish gaseous smoke continued to pour out of the ventilators and machine shop hatch, amidship. After the big explosion and 'swish,' the men painfully burned and wounded, dazed beyond comprehension, came out on the quarterdeck and I had to stop some of them from entering the flames later on, and directed them over to the starboard side of the deck to the gangway for embarking and encouraging them to be calm.

"The *Vestal,* tied up alongside the port side, did not seem to get hit hard and started to get underway."

Actually, crewmen had been abandoning the doomed *Arizona*, now resting on the bottom, for more than two hours even as some machine guns continued to fire at the enemy. The battleship was a coffin for the dead and dying. Marine Corporal Earl C. Nightingale watched "the badly burned men . . . heading for the quarterdeck only to fall apparently dead or badly wounded . . . Charred bodies were everywhere." One man sat on deck blankly staring at the stump where once had been a leg. "I made my way to the quay and started to remove my shoes when I suddenly found myself in the water." He would reflect, "How ridiculous! I am young and have so much to live for!"

He almost did not make it ashore: "My strength gave out entirely, my clothes and shocked condition sapped my strength and I was about to go under when Major [Alan] Shapley [senior member of the Marine detachment] started to swim by, and seeing my distress, he grasped my shirt and told me to hang to his shoulders while he swam in. We were perhaps twenty-five feet from the pipe line [on Ford Island] when the major's strength gave out and I saw he was floundering, so I loosed my grip on him and told him to make it alone.

"He stopped and grabbed me by the shirt and refused to let go. I would have drowned but for the major. We finally reached the beach where a Marine directed us to a bomb shelter."

Another Marine, Sergeant John M. Baker, witnessed this struggle as he himself struck out for shore. He also looked back to see Fuqua still on deck and directing men "shocked too badly to move to abandon ship." He added, "There is no doubt in my mind that many men could never have reached safety except for the superb manner in which he kept control of the situation . . . [He] refused to leave the ship as long as he could help the men who were injured."

Ensign H. D. Davison went into the water, like others, to escape the flames. "I was conscious of a sweetish, sickening smell to the flame. After I got in the water, my first intention was to go to the key and then onto the quarterdeck or swim to the gangway and get aboard. But after I took one look at the ship, I decided that it was useless, she had settled down by the bow and appeared broken in two. The foremast was toppled over; she was a mass of flames from the forecastle to just forward of Turret 3. I was helped into a motor launch."

Ensign Miller concluded his report to the last Sunday morning of the USS *Arizona:* "Our boats which were tied up to the quays and booms were manned by some of the men who had swum to them from the side of the ship. One of the first which came alongside was a motor launch from the *Solace* with a medical rescue party. This boat took all our stretcher cases off the quarterdeck.

"Most of the men who were burned were unrecognizable. Shortly after the stretcher cases had been removed to the *Solace* motor launch, the first lieutenant ordered abandon ship [an order which apparently was given several times by different officers]. All of our guns had ceased firing, the main forecastle and boat decks were burning; smoke obstructed a view of the foremast and the forward part of the ship. All officers' quarters aft were flooded and the quarterdeck forward was awash.

"Our life rafts were cut down and put into the water and all hands ordered to go over the side. Men found the rafts difficult to paddle, and most of them crawled aboard motor launches or started swimming toward Ford Island. The first lieutenant and about half a dozen men and myself were the last to leave in one of our 50-foot motor launches.

"We picked up quite a few more men who were swimming toward the island . . . All hands went ashore except the boat crew . . . We went to the air raid shelter at the northeastern corner of the island."

From the stern of the charred, twisted *Arizona* the Stars and Stripes still flew.

Out of some 1,400 on board, 1,103 officers and men of the

Arizona perished that December 7. The entire band, unofficial winner of the previous night, died. The Navy lost a total of 2,036, the Marines 109. An additional 800 men belonging to the sister services were wounded.

The Army sustained 218 deaths and 364 wounded. There were 68 civilian dead and 35 wounded. Eighteen ships were sunk or badly damaged; 188 planes, about evenly divided between Army and Navy, were destroyed and 160 more damaged. The cost to the Japanese was 29 planes, 5 midget submarines, and 64 men.

Yet of the eight battleships sunk or damaged, only the *Arizona* and *Utah* were not refloated. The others except for the capsized and badly hurt *Oklahoma* were put back in commission. Two, the *Maryland* and the *Pennsylvania*, which had been in drydock, were made seaworthy by the end of December.

Of the many medals and citations bestowed as a result of heroism during the sneak attack, Admiral Kidd and Captain Van Valkenburgh received the highest, the Medal of Honor—posthumously.

It was truly a day, as President Roosevelt was to describe to a joint session of Congress on Monday morning, December 8, "which will live in infamy." It also became something more; "Remember Pearl Harbor!" would be a clarion call, a rallying cry to take its place in history beside the Concord Bridge and the Alamo, John Brown's Body, the *Maine*, and the *Lusitania*. And an integral part was in the blood and sacrifice of those aboard the *Arizona* which had suffered so disproportionately.

President Truman, for one, never forgot. When queried if he ever regretted dropping the atomic bomb, he would riposte, "What about those boys down on the *Arizona*?"

Today, visitors to the marble monument astride the wreck of the nation's most famous and sacred battleship can stare at the outlines of the hull and turrets, just awash, while oil still bubbles intermittently to the surface, at once a reminder of unconscionable perfidy and apathy, and a mute warning to generations unborn.

Author's Note: The December 7 attack on Pearl Harbor is possibly the most voluminously chronicled episode in United States history, rivalled only by that following the assassinations of Presidents Lincoln and Kennedy. For that matter, blank pages persist concerning all three tragedies. This chapter is not an attempt to reconstruct the full fabric of that day of "infamy," but rather to focus on one battleship whose very name became an indelible symbol of what the Nation was fighting for. Nearly 80 percent of those aboard the fated flagship perished. The account is presented largely through the "after action" reports of certain of those who managed to survive, many of which are printed for the first time. Risking the inevitability of some repetition, their recollections are largely unedited in the interest of historical immediacy.

Epilogue

The Liberty Ships

A total of 2,770 Liberty ships were constructed during World War II, about half of the U.S. wartime merchant vessels built. They not only carried cargo to the world's far-flung fighting fronts, but made the beachheads along with the assault forces. The war could scarcely have been waged without them.

The naval Armed Guard crews perished alongside their civilian shipmates—a total of 1,810 dead and missing from 710 merchant ships lost. Approximately 6,000 merchant crewmen out of a quarter million lost their lives.

This phase of World War II, so essential to victory and yet strangely relegated to a background, is told in *The Fighting Liberty Ships*, by A. A. Hoehling (Kent State University Press, 1990). The author, as a naval gunnery officer, served on two Liberty ships and one tanker and was himself a survivor.

Thus, the Liberty ships, too, undeniably helped to change history.

Select Bibliography

Chapter One

The Clippers

Angel, Captain W. H. *The Clipper Ship* Sheila. Boston: Charles E. Lauriat Co., 1923.

Bray, Mary Matthews. *A Sea Trip in Clipper Ship Days*. Boston: Richard G. Badger, The Gorham Press, 1920.

Clark, Arthur H. *The Clipper Ship Era*. New York: G.P. Putnam's Sons, 1910.

Cutler, Carl C. *Greyhounds of the Sea*. New York: G.P. Putnam's Sons, 1930.

Cook, Elliott. *Land Ho!* Baltimore: Remington-Putnam Book Co., 1935.

Hoehling, A. A. *Epics of the Sea*. Chicago: Contemporary Books, 1977.

______. *Great Ship Disasters*. New York: Cowles Books Co., 1971.

Lewis, Oscar. *Sea Routes to the Gold Fields*. New York: Alfred A. Knopf, 1949.

Low, Captain Charles P. *Some Recollections*. Boston: George H. Ellis Co., 1906.

Low, Garrett. *Gold Rush by Sea*. Philadelphia: University of Pennsylvania Press, 1941.

Northrop, Lieutenant Everett H., ed. *Florence Nightingale of the Ocean*. (an account of Mary Patten's assuming command of her husband's clipper, *Neptune's Car*). King's Point, N.Y.: U.S. Merchant Marine Academy, 1959.

Ramsay, Robert. *Rough and Tumble on old Clipper Ships*. New York: D. Appleton & Co., 1930.

Whipple, A. B. C., and the Editors of Time-Life Books. *The Clipper Ships*. Alexandria, Va.: Time-Life Books, 1980.

Chapter Two

The *Great Eastern*

Beaver, Patrick. *The Big Ship*. London: Hugh Evelyn, 1969.

Dugan, James. *The Great Iron Ship*. New York: Harper Bros., 1953.

Farr, Grahame. *The Steamship* Great Western, The First Atlantic Liner. Bristol, England: F. Barber & Son, 1963.

Field, Henry M. *History of the Atlantic Telegram*. New York: Scribner, 1867.

Forwood, Sir William B. *Recollections of a Busy Life*. Liverpool: Henry Young & Sons, 1911.

Noble, Celia Brunel. *The Brunels, Father and Son*. London: Cobden-Sanderson, 1938.

Russell, William H. *The Atlantic Telegraph*. London: Day, 1866.

Strong, George Templeton. *Diary of the Civil War, 1860–1865*. Edited by Allan Nevins. New York: Macmillan, 1962.

"The *Great Eastern* and the Cable." *Atlantic Monthly*, November 1865.

Leslie's Illustrated Weekly and the *Illustrated London News* are referenced in the text. The latter rather faithfully chronicled the entire long career of the *Great Eastern*, as did *The Times* of London. These are to be found in the Library of Congress as well as other newspapers and magazines of the times treating the extraordinary steamship, together with various pamphlets. Her American visits were covered in many East Coast newspapers, some of which are mentioned in the text.

Chapter Three

The *Monitor*

Baldwin, Hanson. *Sea Fights and Shipwrecks.* New York: Hanover House, 1955.

Beach, Captain Edward L. *The Wreck of the* Memphis. New York: Holt, Rinehart & Winston, 1966.

Brown, Cecil. *Suez to Singapore.* New York: Random House, 1942.

Church, William Conant. *The Life of John Ericsson.* New York: Charles Scribner's Sons, 1890.

Dorr, Even P. *A Brief Sketch of the First* Monitor *and its Inventor.* Buffalo, N.Y.: Printing House of Matthews & Warren, 1874.

Hoehling, A. A. *Damn the Torpedoes!: Naval Incidents of the Civil War.* Winston-Salem, N.C.: John F. Blair, 1989.

______. *Thunder at Hampton Roads.* Englewood Cliffs, N.J.: Prentice-Hall, 1976.

Hough, Richard. Dreadnought: *The History of Modern Battleships.* New York: Macmillan, 1964.

Howarth, David, and the Editors of Time-Life Books. *Dreadnoughts.* Alexandria, Va.: Time-Life Books, 1979.

Miller, Nathan. *U.S. Navy: An Illustrated History.* New York: American Heritage Publishing Co. and Naval Institute Press, 1977.

Selfridge, Thomas O. *Memoirs.* New York: G. P. Putnam's Sons, 1924.

Shippen, Dr. Edward S. *Thirty Years at Sea.* Philadelphia: Lippincott Co., 1879.

U.S. Navy. Naval History Division. *Monitors of the U.S. Navy.* Washington, D.C.: Government Printing Office, 1969.

Welles, Gideon. *Diary of Gideon Welles.* Cambridge, Mass.: Houghton Mifflin, 1911.

Worden, John Lorimer. *The* Monitor *and the* Merrimac: *Both Sides of the Story. Told by Lt. J.L. Worden, USN, Lt. Greene, USN of the Monitor, and H. Ashton Ramsay, CSN, Chief Engineer of the Merrimac.* New York and London: Harper & Brothers, 1912.

Young, Brigadier Peter. *The World Almanac Book of World War II.* New York: World Almanac Publications, 1981.

Chapter Four

The *Lusitania*

Bernard, Oliver P. *Cock Sparrow.* London: Jonathan Cape, 1936.

Hoehling, A. A. and Mary Hoehling. *The Last Voyage of the* Lusitania. New York: Henry Holt & Co., 1956.

Hoehling, A. A. *Epics of the Sea.* Chicago: Contemporary Books, 1977.

______. *The Fierce Lambs.* Boston: Little Brown, 1960.

______. *The Great War at Sea.* New York: Crowell, 1965.

______. *Lost at Sea.* Harrisburg, Pa.: Stackpole, 1984.

______. *A Whisper of Eternity.* New York: Yoseloff, 1957.

Millis, Walter. *The Road to War.* Boston: Hougton Mifflin, 1935.

The National Archives contains an extensive Department of State file on the *Lusitania,* including official correspondence and letters from survivors. Elsewhere in this great national depository is a U.S. Signal Corps motion picture of the vessel's last sailing. A number on board, including Captain Turner and Elbert Hubbard, are clearly identifiable.

Chapter Five

The Ships of Dunkirk

Chatterton, E. Keble. *The Epic of Dunkirk.* New York: Viking, 1982.

Churchill, Winston S. *The Second World War. Vol. 2. Their Finest Hour.* Boston: Houghton Mifflin Co., 1949.

Divine, David. *Dunkirk.* New York: E.P. Dutton, 1948.

______. *The Nine Days of Dunkirk.* New York: Norton, 1959.

Jackson, Robert. *Dunkirk: The British Evacuation 1940.* New York: St. Martin's Press, 1976.

Lord, Walter. *The Miracle of Dunkirk.* New York: Viking, 1982.

Paddle Steamer Preservation Society. *Story of the* Medway Queen, *a Paddle Steamer that Went to War.* London: Paddle Steamer Preservation Society, 1975.

Shirer, William L. *The Rise and Fall of the Third Reich.* New York: Simon & Schuster, 1960.

This chapter is based primarily on the vast research, including personal interviews, done by the author in England, especially at the Imperial War Museum, London, for a comprehensive chapter in his book, *Epics of the Sea,* published in 1977 by Contemporary Books, Chicago.

Chapter Six

USS *Arizona*

Army Times Editors. *Pearl Harbor and Hawaii: A Military History.* New York: Walker & Co., 1971.

Hoehling, A. A. *The Week Before Pearl Harbor.* New York: W. W. Norton & Co., 1963.

Layton, Rear Admiral Edwin T. *And I Was There.* New York: William Morrow & Co., 1985.

Lord, Walter. *Day of Infamy.* New York: Rinehart & Co., 1957.

Prange, Gordon. *At Dawn We Slept: The Untold Story of Pearl Harbor.* New York: McGraw-Hill Book Co., 1981.

______. *December 7, 1941.* New York: McGraw-Hill Book Co., 1988.

Thorpe, Brigadier General Elliott R. *East Wind Rain.* Boston: Gambit, 1969.

U.S. Navy. Naval Historical Center. *History of USS* Arizona. Typescript. Washington, D.C.: undated.

The eyewitness reports from survivors of the *Arizona* have been selected from a larger collection of declassified documents made available through the courtesy of Dr. Dean C. Allard, Director of Naval History, Department of the Navy, and Bernard F. Cavalcante, Head, Operational Archives Branch.